IMAGES
of America

FILIPINOS IN
LOS ANGELES

The Filipino Community of Los Angeles, Inc.

Invites You and Your Friends to the

FINAL TABULATION

Queen Candidates for "Miss Philippines" of 1967

SATURDAY, JUNE 10th, 1967 at 8:00 P.M.

KNIGHTS OF COLUMBUS HALL . . . 850 So. Bonnie Brae, Los Angeles, Calif.

LETICIA M. BAUTISTA
71,000 Votes

MARLENE SANTA ANA
37,500 Votes

FELY VITENTE
35,800 Votes

Regular Meeting of the FCLA

SUNDAY, JUNE 18th, 1967 at 3:00 P.M.

FILIPINO CULTURAL CENTER
1740 West Temple Street, Los Angeles

ANNUAL PICNIC

SUNDAY, JULY 2nd, 1967

HAZARD PARK . . . 10 A.M. to 5 P.M.

FREE Hot Dogs and Soft Drinks for the Children
GAMES, BABY CONTEST. Prizes Given Away, Etc.

TESSIE DEL ROSARIO
35,400 Votes

BARBARA ABELLA
11,600 Votes

FOURTH OF JULY MOTORCADE TO CITY HALL

Start Promptly at 10:00 A.M. in Front of the Community Hall

8:00 P.M. — Coronation and Grand Ball, Hollywood Palladium

In celebration of Philippine Independence Day, the Filipino Community of Los Angeles, Inc. (known today as FACLA) sponsored an annual Miss Philippine Pageant to raise money for the community. Featured in this poster are the final candidates from 1967.

ON THE COVER: Hundreds of Filipino Angelenos gather at the Hollywood Palladium for a Grand Independence Day Ball and Coronation of the Queen on July 4, 1962. For more information about the event, see pages 74 and 75.

IMAGES
of America

FILIPINOS IN
LOS ANGELES

Mae Respicio Koerner

ARCADIA
PUBLISHING

Published by Arcadia Publishing
Charleston SC, Chicago IL, Portsmouth NH, San Francisco CA

Library of Congress Catalog Card Number: 2006938519

For all general information contact Arcadia Publishing at:
Telephone 843-853-2070
Fax 843-853-0044
E-mail sales@arcadiapublishing.com
For customer service and orders:
Toll-Free 1-888-313-2665

Visit us on the Internet at www.arcadiapublishing.com

Mae Respicio Koerner is a second-generation Filipina American who has worked on various projects within the entertainment and nonprofit sectors, including for such businesses and organizations as NBC, Nickelodeon, Disney, and UCLA. She is a recipient of a PEN Rosenthal Emerging Voices Fellowship in creative writing and is at work on her first novel. For more information about upcoming projects, visit www.maerespicio.com.

CONTENTS

Acknowledgments   6

Foreword   7

Introduction   8

1.   Filipino Angelenos in the 1920s and 1930s   9

2.   A Glimpse of the 1940s and 1950s   21

3.   Community Life in the 1960s   57

4.   Challenges, Achievements, and Everyday Moments
from the 1970s to Today   83

Bibliography   127

ACKNOWLEDGMENTS

Filipinos in Los Angeles would not have been possible without the help of numerous individuals and organizations. I wish I had room here to list their complete bios—they each bring great pride to the community through their expertise, care, and contributions.

I am grateful to those who lent me their resources: Cat Avendano; Joseph Bernardo, field deputy for Historic Filipinotown; Eloisa Borah, UCLA librarian; longtime Angeleno Nena Calica; Dorothy Cordova, executive director of the Filipino American National Historical Society (FANHS); community leader Johann Diel; Dr. Linda España-Maram, professor of Asian American studies at Long Beach State University; author Jessica Hagedorn; Joel Jacinto, executive director of Search to Involve Pilipino Americans (SIPA); Irwin Jazmines, member of the Philippine Press Photographers; Frances Lacebal, retired educator and one of the original members of the Filipino American Educators Association of L.A.; Carmella Leelin of the Goldilocks family; Zen Lopez, arts and culture commissioner for the City of Glendale; Erick Mata, principal of Marina del Rey Middle School; R. Sonny Sampayan, grandnephew of writer Carlos Bulosan; business owner Maria Skiles; and Phil Ventura of FANHS-L.A. and a longtime Angeleno.

I am indebted to those who enthusiastically opened their homes and businesses (and sometimes dining rooms), shared their wisdom and memories, and lent their time and photographs to this effort: commander of the Veterans Center Association and retired educator Lourdes "Lulu" Astilla; Jay Africa, of East West Players; student and father of triplets Ron Albino; designer Gina Alexander; author Noel Alumit; actress Jennifer Aquino; animator Ruben Aquino; author Cecilia Manguerra Brainard; longtime member of the Filipino Christian Church Hermenia Balderama; young community activist Loralei Rose Bingamon; retired educator Chris Campos; longtime member of the Philippine Women's Group Elnora Campos; director of Silayan Dance Company Dulce Capadocia; artist Ray Carbudillo; photographer Karlo David; actress Liza Del Mundo; former member of the U.S. Navy Reserves, judicial assistant, and L.A. native Carina Monica Montoya-Forsythe; owner of Remy's on Temple Jocelyn Geaga-Rosenthal; filmmaker Patricio Ginelsa; longtime Angeleno Tawa Desuacido; retired educator Lucila Dypiangco; Reme Grefalda, editor of *Our Own Voices*; manager of Library Computer Services at Loyola Law School Florante Peter Ibañez; community leader Benita Q. Lagmay; photographer Shatto Light; Jeff Liu of Visual Communications; Jonathan Lorenzo, administrator of the Filipino American Library; Vanessa Vela Lovelace, of Fil Am ARTS; photographer Vics Magsaysay; filmmaker Edward J. Mallillin; actress Ronalee Par Miyasaki; Kelly Mohnkern of Duncan Toys; owner of Philippine Expressions Bookshop Linda Nietes; Arnold A. Noche of All Things Filipino; Mary-Ann Ortiz-Luis, president of Clarmil Manufacturing and part of the Goldilocks family; photographer Ernie Peña; nurse Jennifer Respicio; director Jon Lawrence Rivera; James Saspa, editor of *Balita Magazine*; muralist Eliseo Art Silva; artist Celina Taganas-Duffy; businessman Chito Tenza; Meg Malpaya Thorton, of the UCLA Asian American Studies Center; and photographer Apollo Victoria.

Thank you to my editor at Arcadia Publishing, Jerry Roberts, for his desire to publish this book and his expert guidance, and to Scott Davis of Arcadia for all of his help with images.

My appreciation to Carolyn Kozo Cole, senior librarian, Photograph Collections/History and Genealogy Department of the Los Angeles Public Library for her support of the book and use of images from the Shades of L.A. collection. I would also like to thank Mark Pulido, member of the Board of Education of ABC Unified School District, and Melissa Pulido Rebaya—both have lent their energy and resources, and I am inspired by their passion and knowledge. Finally, my gratitude to the Honorable Casimiro U. Tolentino for graciously providing his time, longtime community experiences, and voice to writing the book's foreword.

I also wish to thank my parents, Restie and Tina Respicio, and the Respicio family (Stockton and Los Angeles) for their love; to my grandfather Franky T. Respicio for encouraging my writing, and to my husband, Mark, for helping me with Photoshop and being the most supportive one of all.

FOREWORD

About 35 years ago at UCLA, I attended my first Asian American Experience class. The time spent on Pilipino American history was only one lecture, but I learned more about my own heritage in that brief hour than in 15 years of schooling. The professor stated that he wished he had more but was limited on what literature was available at that time. The class planted a seed that germinated into a lifelong interest in ensuring that our experiences and stories would be told and documented.

Facing this challenge, I helped cofound UCLA Samahang Pilipino, a student group focused on advocating the interests of Pilipino students, and developed and taught at UCLA the first Pilipino experience class, America's Little Brown Brother: The Pilipino American Experience in California. Like two years earlier, the available literature was minimal; I used copies of old Ph.D. theses, excerpts from articles, and excerpts from books of Filipino writers Carlos Bulosan and Manuel Buaken. Bulosan's novel at that time was not reprinted, and much information came from guest lecturers such as Phillip Vera Cruz and Larry Itliong, speaking of their experiences in the farmworkers' movement. *Letters in Exile*, an anthology based on writings by my UCLA students, was collected in one of the earliest published works on the Pilipino American experience.

I was not a historian, but a law student who went on to work in the fields of California—as an attorney for the California Agricultural Labor Relations Board. In the small towns of California's central valley, I continued to learn more about Pilipinos and their lives. I learned of the Native American/Filipino community in Sonora, the Hispanic/Filipinos in Coachella and El Centro, and the continuing immigrants to Delano and Bakersfield, but no one was writing and documenting their stories. One common tradition of our communities was that we all took photographs, from Polaroids to Kodak and home movie cameras. Our stories were documented in images of fiestas, baptisms, provincial dinner dances, and everyday activities. These family treasures provide the context for much of our experience surviving and overcoming prejudice and racism in California.

Today we still see a lack of documentation of our history, but this book provides a bridge of academic research and experiential knowledge and contributes to the gathering knowledge of our communities and lives. I see in snapshots of Boy Scout ceremonies my own son; I see in the images of baptisms and confirmations my own children; and I see in the dinner dances a reflection of my parents maintaining cultural ties in a new place. The photographs of community demonstrations for Pilipino veterans, for Pilipino farmworkers, and for equal opportunity resonate with my own experiences. This book will hopefully galvanize all of us to document our lives and experiences in the fabric of American history. The old maxim that we need to remember the past to move forward with the future bodes well in this book.

—The Honorable Casimiro Urbano Tolentino
Los Angeles, California

INTRODUCTION

In his 1943 semiautobiographical novel *America is in the Heart*, Filipino writer and poet Carlos Bulosan wrote, "I reached Los Angeles in the evening. An early autumn rain was falling. I waited in the station, looking among the passengers for Filipino faces. Then I went out and turned northward on Los Angeles Street, and suddenly familiar signs on barbershops and restaurants came to view. I felt as though I had discovered a new world. I entered a restaurant and heard the lonely sound of my dialect, the soft staccato of home. I knew at once that I would meet some people I had known in the Philippines."

I first discovered Bulosan's writing in my early 20s. I remember the questions it brought about for me: who were the early Filipino immigrants and what were their stories? My great-grandfather Francisco Ila came to the United States in 1930 where he first worked as a *sakada* in the sugarcane fields of Hawaii before heading to the Los Angeles area, where he later became one of Shirley Temple's drivers. Unfortunately, my family does not have photographs of his experiences. Still, I have always wondered what coming to a new country must have been like for him, in a setting where immigrants of his time were met by signs that read, "Positively No Filipinos Allowed."

While studying journalism in college, I was always taught to ask questions, and this book was an opportunity to do just that. As of the 2000 U.S. Census there were 260,158 people of Filipino ancestry in Los Angeles County. Who are the people that make up this incredible number? Where do they reside? What are their jobs? How do they live? There are thousands of Filipino American voices in Los Angeles, and I wish I could include all of them here. However, this book serves as merely a starting point in sharing just a few of their unique stories, perhaps also inspiring others to further explore their family's personal history.

Photographs act as proof of existence, as glimpses into others' lives, and as opportunities to leave legacies. The images in these pages were collected from a variety of individuals and organizations, and many taken straight from the sleeves of family albums. They answer the questions about what Filipino Americans have contributed to the community, what challenges they have faced, and, as Filipino Angelenos, what we do in our everyday moments.

—Mae Respicio Koerner
Los Angeles, California

One

FILIPINO ANGELENOS IN THE 1920S AND 1930S

Mrs. J. V. ABELLA

Published in English, Spanish and Filipino.   TEN CENTS

In 1920, the U.S. Census reported that there was a population of 5,603 Filipino Americans living in the United States. The majority of Filipinos during this first, substantial wave of immigrants were unmarried young men, most of whom were *manongs*—migratory laborers who worked in rural agricultural areas. Others migrated to urban areas like Los Angeles and worked in such service-oriented jobs as houseboys, porters, and janitors. A small group of these Filipinos was also known as "fountain pen boys," self-supporting students who attended Southern California colleges while also working in service positions. In Los Angeles, the first large wave of Filipinos settled in small enclaves around the impoverished downtown area between Main and Los Angeles Streets—the only pocket in the city they were allowed to rent in due to discrimination—and it was known as Little Manila (today the area is designated as Little Tokyo). Filipinos traveled there in search of housing, work, and social networks to connect them with their home country. Pictured here is the cover of a Los Angeles–based publication called the *Philippine Progress*, published by the fraternal order Caballeros de Dimas-Alang. This issue featured the headlines, "Our Xmas Gift From Coolidge," which reported on the new governor-general of the Philippines and "The Coming Great Event," which excitedly informed readers about the "1927 Pacific Coast Joint Rizal Day Celebration." The publication shared news about fraternal and social organizations, local businesses, work, and housing opportunities and had recreational ads for dance halls and billiard rooms, as well as news from the Philippines. In this issue, the Philippine Employment Agency advertised: "We furnish all kinds of help on short notice." The Liberty Dancing Pavilion on East Third Street called itself "The Palace of Enjoyment where Filipinos Like to Dance . . . Dancing Every Night Except Sundays." (Courtesy of the Filipino American Library.)

9

CERTIFICATE OF MEDICAL EXAMINATION AND IDENTITY
ISSUED BY
U. S. PUBLIC HEALTH SERVICE
QUARANTINE SERVICE, MANILA, P. I.

4521

No N 1503

Passenger's Name:
Citizen of Philippine Islands *Silvestre Morales*

Name of ship from Manila: *Empress of Canada*
Date of departure from Manila: *June 8, 1928*
Connecting Hongkong with S. S.: *Tenyu Maru*
Sailing from Hongkong: *June 12, 1928*
For: *Los Angeles, U.S.A.*
Bacteriologically negative or cholera:
Date: JUN 7 1928
Vaccinated against small pox:
Date: JUN 4 1928

Surgeon, U. S. P. H. S.

In 1928, Silvestre Morales's long boat trip began in Manila, stopped in Hong Kong, and eventually ended in Los Angeles. In the 1930s, Morales eventually became reverend of the Filipino Christian Church, which provided support for the mostly young, single, male Filipino immigrants who came to Los Angeles in search of economic and educational opportunities. (Courtesy of Shades of L.A. Archives/Los Angeles Public Library.)

A group of travelers aboard a ship awaits the journey to a new country in 1927. Helen Summers Brown, whose mother was Filipina, is pictured third from left with her father, George Robert Summers (far left). Brown became an educator in the Los Angeles Unified School District and is the founder of the Filipino American Library, currently located in Historic Filipinotown. (Courtesy of Shades of L.A. Archives/Los Angeles Public Library.)

10

First-generation immigrants and "town mates," or those who came from the same province, village, or town in the Philippines, pose for a photograph in the Los Angeles Harbor area during the 1930s. The men, including Romy Madirgal, standing second from right; Dodo Zamorano, standing second from left; and Bonifacio Libre, seated center, worked in the fish canneries on nearby Terminal Island. (Courtesy of Shades of L.A. Archives/Los Angeles Public Library.)

Filipino Angelenos gather at First and Hope Streets in downtown Los Angeles, c. 1930. (Courtesy of Shades of L.A. Archives/Los Angeles Public Library.)

Little

Manila Times

EQUAL JUSTICE UNDER LAW

"A PRODUCER A DEFENDER"

"Official Organ of all Filipinos Abroad"

LOS ANGELES, CALIFORNIA

FILIPINO STUDENTS TO GRADUATE WITH HIGH HONORS

Jose B. Baldivino, A.B.

Severino Corpus, M.A.

Alfonso P. Santos, M.S.

COMMENCEMENT EXERCISES

U. S. C. — May 20th
Coliseum

Cal'f. Ass'ted Colleges June 3
960 So. Flower St.

Occidental College,, June 6th
Greek Bowl

U. C. L. A. — June 11th
Hollywood Bowl

Loyola University - June 12th
Playa del Rey

Note: Read local papers for
other commencements.

Amador Gonong, A.B.

Grogorio Minodin, A.B., LL.B.

A group of Filipino graduates is pictured here in the late 1930s. The front page of the *Manila Times*, which was printed in Los Angeles, listed Filipino graduates of such schools as the University of Southern California, Occidental College, and Loyola Marymount University. For his 1938 USC thesis, Severino Corpus wrote the paper, "An Analysis of the Racial Adjustment Activities and Problems of the Filipino-American Christian Fellowship in Los Angeles," examining the influence of the organization upon the lives of Filipino youth. In his conclusion, Corpus stated, "Man is the only living being that has nowhere been content merely to live; he has wanted to live with rich experience. Therefore, the leader in character development must help a group find and set forth principles that enrich social and personal experience; he must discover, arrange, and capitalize situations in which the principles may be practiced; and he must be open-minded in the critical evaluation of principles commonly accepted." (Courtesy of Hermenia Balderama.)

Reverend C. Coloma (right) sits with friends outside the Los Angeles Public Library, *c.* 1930. The friends include Epifania Morales (second from right) and her daughter Edith. (Courtesy of Shades of L.A. Archives/Los Angeles Public Library.)

Genaro Manantan (right) and a friend pose for a picture in downtown Los Angeles in the 1930s. (Courtesy of Shades of L.A. Archives/Los Angeles Public Library.)

Camilo Serrano serves bridge players at a card table around 1938. Like other "fountain pen boys" of the 1920s and 1930s, Serrano attended school while working in a self-supporting, service-oriented position; he was a student at the University of Southern California. (Courtesy of Shades of L.A. Archives/Los Angeles Public Library.)

Filipino American pilots gather at the Santa Monica Airport around 1930. Genaro Manantan is standing at center. (Courtesy of Shades of L.A. Archives/Los Angeles Public Library.)

Pictured here on August 24, 1933, are some of the newly elected officers of the National Society Army of the Philippines during a convention at the Los Angeles Alexandria Hotel, in connection with the national convention of the United Spanish War Veterans. (Courtesy of Shades of L.A. Archives/Los Angeles Public Library.)

Mariano Dahilig (seated at left), a graduate of the University of Southern California, poses with a friend for a photograph to send home to relatives in the Philippines. (Courtesy of Hermenia Balderama.)

1927 Pacific Coast Joint Rizal Day Celebration

POPULARITY CONTEST

TO BE HELD AT LOS ANGELES UNDER THE AUSPICES OF THE LUNA
LODGE NO. 8 (C. D. A. INC.) WITH THE COOPERATION OF VARIOUS
FILIPINO ORGANIZATIONS IN THE PACIFIC COAST

VOTE FOR

GOOD FOR 100 VOTES

CONTEST CLOSES MIDNIGHT DECEMBER 24, 1927
CLIP THIS COUPON AND MAIL TO

DEC. 15

CHAIRMAN — POPULARITY CONTEST
142 WELLER ST.

This ad is taken from the *Philippine Progress*, a weekly magazine that cost 10¢ per copy. An article about the 1927 Pacific Coast Joint Rizal Day Celebration shares, "Filipinos will begin to arrive in Los Angeles to witness the greatest celebration ever tendered to the honor and memory of The Great Patriot and Martyr. Flags and banners will be weaving in the streets. The 24th ends at the Veteran's Hall the Popularity Contest which is the hottest ever seen around this part of the Country. The Queen will be crowned on the 29th in the most beautiful Auditorium in California, the Ambassador's of Los Angeles and the following day . . . in the afternoon will be the parade where numerous artistic and expensive floats will be seen in the City's main streets." The article ends with, "The whole success is due to the cooperation of all Filipino organizations, societies, brotherhoods, fraternal orders, in the United States. It is once more demonstrated that together we win and succeed." (Courtesy of the Filipino American Library.)

Pedro Flores is known as the inventor of the popular toy called the yo-yo, which means "come-come" in the national Filipino language of Tagalog. Flores immigrated to the United States in the 1920s and worked as a bellhop at a Santa Monica hotel. During lunch breaks, he played with his invention, often drawing a crowd. Eventually he started the Flores Yo-Yo Company. Pictured here is one of his original toys. (Courtesy of Duncan Toys/Flambeau, Inc.)

A group of young men formed the Los Angeles Filipino basketball team around 1928. (Courtesy of Photographic Collections, Visual Communications.)

Pictured here on September 17, 1932, are members of an early fraternal organization called the Knights of the Cross. (Courtesy of Photographic Collections, Visual Communications.)

In 1937, members of the University of Southern California's Philippines Trojan Club are seated for dinner. While further details about this particular club are unknown, today the Troy Philippines Club at USC is a student-run organization that educates students and the community about the Filipino culture through various events. (Courtesy of Shades of L.A. Archives/Los Angeles Public Library.)

This issue of the *Philippine Society Year Book of Southern California* is dated December 12, 1931, and lists general member gatherings, including luncheons, teas, and dinners in such locations as Griffith Park and The Jonathan Club in downtown Los Angeles. (Courtesy of the Filipino American Library.)

YEAR BOOK

PHILIPPINE SOCIETY
of
SOUTHERN CALIFORNIA

DECEMBER TWELFTH, NINETEEN THIRTY-ONE

LOS ANGELES

GENERAL GATHERINGS

1923—Luncheon.......The Log House, Home of Mrs. Clark J. Milliron
1924—Tea.............Home of Mrs. Edward Milham Ayres, Pasadena
1924—Tea........................Home of Mrs. H. Buffington Atkins
1924—First Annual Dinner.............................The Elite
    The First Election
1924—Second Annual Dinner.....................The Mary Louise
    Manila Hemp
1925—Picnic.....................................Brookside Park
1925—Third Annual Dinner.....................The Mary Louise
1926—Picnic..Griffith Park
1926—Fourth Annual Dinner....................The Masonic Club
1927—Cañao..........................El Caballero Country Club
1927—Top Side Fiesta..........The Log House, Home of the President
1927—Fifth Annual Dinner.....................The Masonic Club
    Escula han, 1898
1928—Luncheon, in honor of Mr. and Mrs. Cris O. Hagen
                The Masonic Club
1928—Lechon'.........................The California Country Club
1928—Typhoon Reception, in honor of Rear Admiral and
    Mrs. Sumner E. W. Kittelle
       The Log House, Home of the President and Mrs. Milliron
1928—Sixth Annual Dinner and Dance..............The Masonic Club
    Regidon
1929—Shrine Luncheon..........................The Masonic Club
1929—Elks Luncheon.....................................The Elite
1929—Seventh Annual Dinner and Dance.........The Alexandria Hotel
    El Tiendero
1930—Auction Bridge Party.....................The Shoreham Hotel
1930—Luncheon, in honor of Justice and Mrs. T. A. Street
                The Alexandria Hotel
1930—Banquet and Dance, in honor of His Excellency
    W. Cameron Forbes, American Ambassador to Tokyo, Japan
                The Alexandria Hotel
1930—Eighth Annual Dinner and Dance.........The Alexandria Hotel
1931—Tea, in honor of Vice Governor and Mrs. George C. Butte,
    Philippine Islands.......................The Jonathan Club
1931—N. E. A. Luncheon............................The La Palma
1931—Dinner, in honor of Dr. Bolivar L. Falconer, former Director of
    Civil Service, Philippine Islands................The La Palma
1931—Como Se Llama..............................The Log House
1931—Luncheon, in honor of Mr. Harvey Vaughn Rohrer,
    American Trade Commissioner, Manila..........The La Palma
1931—Ninth Annual Dinner and Frolic..The Masonic Club Dining Room
    Oriental Night

The Fourth Inaugural Banquet and Ball of the Philippine Junior Assembly is depicted in this photograph, taken at the Café de Paree in Los Angeles on March 8, 1936. (Courtesy of Photographic Collections, Visual Communications.)

A group of Filipino Americans gathers in 1938 at an annual banquet of the Cabugao Club, a hometown club from the Philippines. Camilo Serrano was the event's organizer. (Courtesy of Shades of L.A. Archives/Los Angeles Public Library.)

Two

A GLIMPSE OF THE 1940S AND 1950S

The Philippine Declaration of Independence occurred on June 12, 1898, when Filipino revolutionary forces under Gen. Emilio Aguinaldo (later to become the Philippines' first Republican president) proclaimed the sovereignty and independence of the Philippine Islands from the colonial rule of Spain. However, the declaration was not recognized by the United States or Spain, as the Spanish government ceded the Philippines to the United States in the 1898 Treaty of Paris. On July 4, 1946, the United States returned full leadership of the Republic of the Philippines to the Filipino people. In 1940, the U.S. Census listed the Filipino American population at 45,208. By 1950, the number had risen to 61,645. Those who came during these years are often referred to as the second wave of Filipino immigration. After the war, many Filipinos, including professionals and both skilled and unskilled workers, came to the United States in search of work. In Los Angeles, further restrictive covenants, discrimination, and redevelopment of the Little Manila area led many Filipino Angelenos to move farther west into Bunker Hill. An enclave of Filipinos formed in this area from around 1942 through the late 1950s. Despite anti-miscegenation laws, many Filipinos married non-Filipino women, also forcing them to leave the hotel-housing life of Little Manila in search of a more residential life in other parts of the city. The Bunker Hill area once housed wealthy Caucasian families in large Victorian-style homes who moved to suburban subdivisions that prohibited ethnic minorities. Pictured here in 1941 is a group of Filipino Angelenos posing for a novelty photograph. (Courtesy of Photographic Collections, Visual Communications.)

Men play billiards in a downtown Filipino recreational hall located at 245 South Main Street in 1940. The photograph lists the proprietor as Vincent Noble. (Courtesy of Shades of L.A. Archives/Los Angeles Public Library.)

Filipino American youths perform a play titled *The Boy who Found the King* at an annual Christmas festival in the Fellowship Auditorium of the Filipino Christian Church in 1940. The play was directed by Ruperto V. de Castro. (Courtesy of Photographic Collections, Visual Communications.)

Pictured here are moments at the L. V. M. Café, which stood for Luzon, Visayas, and Mindanao, the three primary sections of the Philippines, which is an archipelago consisting of 7,107 islands. The photograph above, taken in the 1940s, shows waitresses (including Tawa Desuacido, standing far left) with restaurant patrons (seated). A menu lists "Cooked to Order" Filipino foods such as *pansit* (Filipino noodles) for 65¢. The café was located at 113 East First Street in downtown Los Angeles. Such Filipino-owned businesses contributed to the daily life of Filipino Angelenos and provided a sense of home and family. (Above courtesy of Tawa Desuacido; below courtesy of Photographic Collections, Visual Communications.)

Pictured here *c.* 1942 is a gathering of the Cabugao Club, a hometown organization. (Courtesy of Shades of L.A. Archives/Los Angeles Public Library.)

A group of Filipinas, many of them second-generation youths of high school age, gets ready to perform traditional Filipino folk dances in the early 1940s, though the exact event is unknown. (Courtesy of Tawa Desuacido.)

Tawa Desuacido is pictured here in 1944 with a friend at Roosevelt High School in East Los Angeles. Born in Ventura, Desuacido, whose mother originally immigrated to Hawaii, remembers being only one of a few Filipinas in her high school. Her grandchildren are now third-generation Filipino Angelenos. (Courtesy of Tawa Desuacido.)

A group of high school friends, including Tony Maravel (far left) and Armando Manalo (far right), are photographed here at Polytechnic High School in Long Beach, c. 1946. The city of Long Beach is located in the southern part of Los Angeles County and, as of the year 2000, had a population of over 18,000 Filipino Americans (about four percent). (Courtesy of Tawa Desuacido.)

Filipino American friends enjoy the sun and waves at Venice Beach during the 1940s. (Courtesy of Carina Monica Montoya-Forsythe.)

Here, in 1945, a group of Filipinas pose for a photograph near the corner of Sunset Boulevard and Main Street in Los Angeles. Second from the left is Ursula Rigor, followed by Juana Noble Manantan, and Evelyn Yaney. (Courtesy of Shades of L.A. Archives/Los Angeles Public Library.)

Like other youth in Los Angeles, Filipino Americans often participated in Hollywood nightlife, visiting clubs and dance halls. The group above enjoys dinner and drinks at Slapsy Maxie's in Hollywood during the 1940s. (Courtesy of Tawa Desuacido.)

Members of the Filipino Christian Church celebrate Mother's Day at an annual banquet and program in 1942 (above) and at a 1945 dinner for their Filipino Youth Club (below). In 1928, thirteen Filipino students from California Christian College, now known as Chapman University, formed the Filipino Christian Fellowship. In 1933, with the help of Reverends Silvestre Morales and Felix Pascua, the fellowship was formally organized into the Filipino Christian Church, which provided refuge from racial prejudice and religious discrimination and served as a religious, social, and recreational group for Filipinos Angelenos, especially those new to the United States. In 1998, the church was designated as Historical Cultural Monument No. 651 by the City of Los Angeles Cultural Heritage Commission and is located today in Historic Filipinotown. (Courtesy of Shades of L.A. Archives/Los Angeles Public Library.)

The Filipino Community of Los Angeles, Inc., celebrates newly elected officials on Easter Sunday in 1949 at a banquet and ball held at the Alexandria Hotel in Los Angeles, California. The hotel itself was built in 1906, and in its earlier years, it became a natural meeting place for the burgeoning film industry, hosting people like Winston Churchill and American presidents Taft, Wilson, and Roosevelt during its heyday. (Courtesy of Photographic Collections, Visual Communications.)

Filipino Angelenos attend the Filipino Federation of America Children's Christmas program on December 24, 1946, at the Symphony Hall in Los Angeles, California. The audience is composed largely of Filipino males, a reflection of earlier immigration patterns. (Courtesy of Shades of L.A. Archives/Los Angeles Public Library.)

Griffith Park was often the location of get-togethers for Filipino American youths, including both of these groups of friends. Both photographs were taken during the 1940s. (Above courtesy of Carina Monica Montoya-Forsythe; below courtesy of Tawa Desuacido.)

Tomas "Tommy" Montoya (seated, fourth from left) and his friends gather in Montoya's apartment, located downtown in Little Manila, the area designated as Little Tokyo today. (Courtesy of Carina Monica Montoya-Forsythe.)

A wedding reception at a Los Angeles home is the setting of this c. 1947 image. Pictured from left to right are Primitivo Labao, stepfather of the bride; the bride, Timi Villahermosa; her groom, Lawrence Refoli; Aqui Villahermosa; and Leon Villahermosa, father of the bride. (Courtesy of Tawa Desuacido.)

A group of Filipino men and soldiers pose for a photograph at a farm in Torrance during the 1940s. Today Torrance is the sixth largest city in Los Angeles County and has about a three percent population of Filipino Americans. (Courtesy of Tawa Desuacido.)

In 1943, a group of Filipino Angelenos came together to raise votes for Marceline Jacobe Cruz, who won the Miss Philippines title of the Los Angeles community that year. Jacobe Cruz is pictured fourth from left in the middle row. (Courtesy of Tawa Desuacido.)

As part of the war-relief efforts, a group of Filipino Angelenos plans a USO dance for around 200 soldiers at Camp Cook. (Courtesy of Tawa Desuacido.)

In connection with the United National Clothing Drive, Los Angeles mayor Fletcher Bowron, center, welcomes a group of leaders from the local Filipino American community in 1945. (Courtesy of Shades of L.A. Archives/Los Angeles Public Library.)

Pictured here are the identification cards of Helen Summers Brown, who worked as a welder during World War II. (Courtesy of Shades of L.A. Archives/Los Angeles Public Library.)

Filipino American servicemen and friends gather in downtown Los Angeles to celebrate the end of World War II in 1945. (Courtesy of Shades of L.A. Archives/Los Angeles Public Library.)

Hollywood actors John Wayne and Anthony Quinn starred in a 1945 movie called *Back to Bataan*, inspired by General MacArthur's withdrawal from the Philippines in 1942 and the islands' subsequent conquest by the Japanese army. Pictured above from left to right are young Filipina Angelenos who were extras in the film: Connie Marasigan Baning, John Wayne (who played Col. Joseph Madden), Tawa Desuacido, Edward Dmytryk (the film's director), Connie Dizon, Marcy Jacobe, Delnia Gersalia, actor Anthony Quinn (who played Capt. Andres Bonifacio), and Jessie Celaya. Below is a school scene from the movie, featuring other Filipino extras. The film, made by RKO Pictures, was shot at studios as well as on location at such places as Seal Beach and the Santa Anita race grounds. (Courtesy of Tawa Desuacido.)

The director of *Back to Bataan*, Edward Dmytryk, sits in between takes of the movie with Filipino American actors who were extras on the film. Some youth from area high schools and colleges were recruited as extras, in addition to the professional Filipino American actors who played bit parts in the movie. Tawa Desuacido recalls being paid $25 a day as an extra. (Courtesy Tawa Desuacido.)

Members of the Filipino Christian Church perform in a play at their annual Christmas pageant in 1955. (Courtesy of Shades of L.A. Archives/Los Angeles Public Library.)

The Filipino Color Guard marches down Los Angeles Street in 1942. (Courtesy of Shades of L.A. Archives/Los Angeles Public Library.)

In the early 1940s, Filipino American Genaro Manantan (standing, face scratched out) worked as a houseboy and chauffeur for Hollywood actress Dorothy Lamour (far left). (Courtesy of Shades of L.A. Archives/Los Angeles Public Library.)

Delegates attend the 23rd Annual National Convention of the Filipino Federation of America (FFA) at the Moncado Mansion in Los Angeles in December 1948. The FFA was formed in Los Angeles in 1925 by Hilario Camino Moncado, a *Cebuano* who worked on Kauai's sugar plantations before moving to Los Angeles. The FFA was a mutual-aid organization that evolved into a messianic movement. Their "office" was the Moncado Mansion, which is still located on Arlington Avenue at 25th Street in the West Adams area of Los Angeles. Moncado's followers believed that he was a prophet. (Courtesy of Shades of L.A. Archives/Los Angeles Public Library.)

Filipino Americans were among those who worked at the Naval Supply Depot in San Pedro, pictured here in March 1946. (Courtesy of Tawa Desuacido.)

Pictured here in 1948 is the Legionarios del Trabajo, an organization founded by early immigrants with roots as a support network for Filipino immigrants; it fostered opportunities to develop leadership and community-development skills. Lodges were established nationally, though today they have dwindled to only a few chapters, including those in California and Washington. (Courtesy of Shades of L.A. Archives/Los Angeles Public Library.)

Here, on February 26, 1949, Filipino Americans dine at the 22nd Inaugural Banquet and Ball of the Pangasinan Association of Southern California, a hometown club, held at the Alexandria Hotel in downtown Los Angeles. (Courtesy of Shades of L.A. Archives/Los Angeles Public Library.)

On April 27, 1947, the marriage of Benita Quibilan to Numeriano D. Lagmay was the first wedding to take place at the St. Columban Filipino Catholic Church's new location in Los Angeles. Below, in celebration of the occasion, family and friends pose for a photograph in front of a Los Angeles home. (Both courtesy of Benita Q. and Numeriano D. Lagmay.)

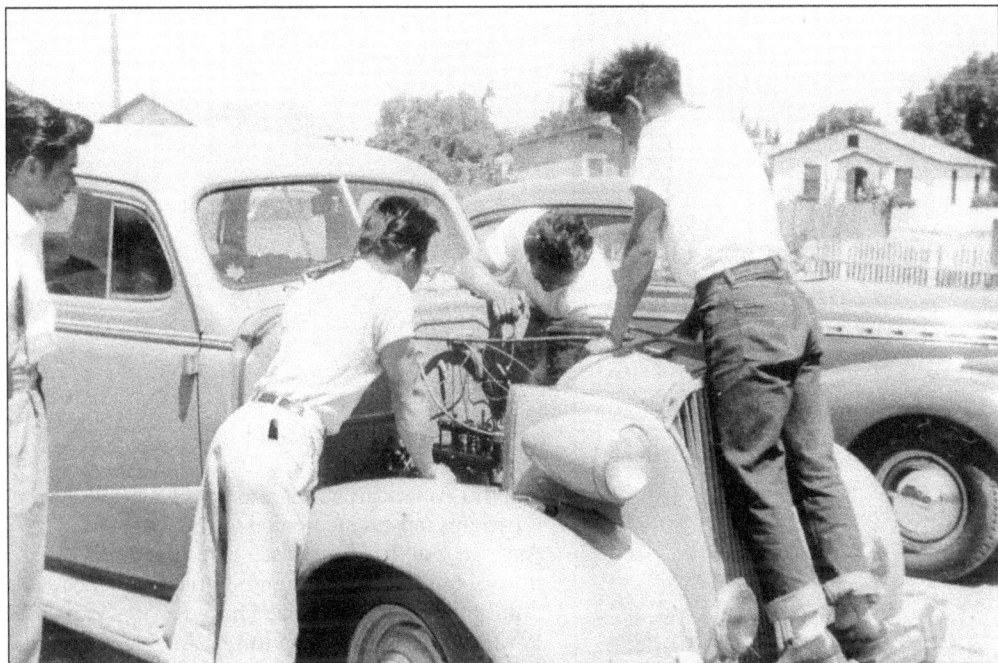

Salvador Palicte (far left) and his friends work on their automobile in Los Angeles in 1949. (Courtesy of Shades of L.A. Archives/Los Angeles Public Library.)

In 1949, Joe Palicte stands in front of the boardinghouse where he lived while attending the National Automotive Trade School. The house was located on Figueroa and Exposition Streets across from the Los Angeles Coliseum. (Courtesy of Shades of L.A. Archives/Los Angeles Public Library.)

Filipino American writer and poet Carlos Bulosan is perhaps most remembered for his 1946 novel *America is in the Heart*, a semiautobiographical story about the Filipino immigrant experience. Bulosan immigrated to the United States in 1930, and during his time in Los Angeles, the self-taught writer reportedly read a book a day. (Courtesy of Reme-Antonia Grefalda, editor of *Our Own Voices*.)

A group of Filipino graduates gathers in front of the Filipino Christian Church in 1951. (Courtesy of Shades of L.A. Archives/Los Angeles Public Library.)

Pictured here are the 1954 graduates of Los Angeles City College, including Natividad Navares Palicte (standing in the third row from the bottom, third from the left). (Courtesy of Shades of L.A. Archives/Los Angeles Public Library.)

The Pangasinan Association of Southern California, Inc., gathers for a dinner dance in 1950 at the Alexandria Hotel in downtown Los Angeles. (Courtesy of Shades of L.A. Archives/Los Angeles Public Library.)

C.D.A. Inc.
Banquet and Ball
Gen. Trias Lodge No. 21 Hollywood, Calif.
Honoring the 1950 Queen of the Philippine Republic,
Alexandria Hotel, Los Angeles, Cal. July 1, 1950

Members of the fraternal organization Caballeros de Dimas-Alang, Inc., attend a banquet and ball honoring the 1950 Queen of the Philippine Republic at the Alexandria Hotel in downtown Los Angeles. (Courtesy of Photographic Collections, Visual Communications.)

FIFTH TABULATION DANCE OF THE NATIONAL
CHAPTER. FILIPINO-AMERICAN CITIZENS INC.
HELD AT PASADENA, CAL. AUGUST 19, 1950

A group comes together for the fifth tabulation dance of the national chapter of Filipino American Citizens, Inc., in Pasadena on August 19, 1950. Pasadena is a city within Los Angeles County and home to the annual Rose Bowl football game and the Tournament of Roses Parade. (Courtesy of Shades of L.A. Archives/Los Angeles Public Library.)

Her Majesty, Queen Gloria II
Miss Philippines of 1950 celebration
of the 2nd Anniversary of the Filipino
American Citizens Inc. November 9, 1950
Los Angeles, Cal. Photo by Clora-Sobrepeña

Pictured here in November 1950 is her majesty, Queen Gloria, Miss Philippines of the organization Filipino American Citizens, Inc. (Courtesy of Shades of L.A. Archives/Los Angeles Public Library.)

Shown here is Amparo Domingo, who was elected as the president of the Filipino Community Association in 1959. (Courtesy of Benita Q. Lagmay and Numeriano D. Lagmay.)

A banquet and ball for the Filipino Alumni Association honored graduates at the Hotel Statler in Los Angeles in July 1953. (Courtesy of Shades of L.A. Archives/Los Angeles Public Library.)

Filipino Americans get ready to dine and dance at the first annual banquet of the Caballeros de Dimas-Alang. The ball took place in 1951 at the Ambassador Hotel in downtown Los Angeles. Such fraternal organizations were established as a result of Filipinos finding white society closed to them. (Courtesy of Shades of L.A. Archives/Los Angeles Public Library.)

Members of the Caballeros de Dimas-Alang, including Numeriano D. Lagmay (center, standing), Fe and Juanita Della (right), Justin Della, and Ben Carreon (kneeling), pose during a dinner event at the Filipino Masonic Lodge Dance in 1953. (Courtesy of Benita Q. and Numeriano D. Lagmay.)

Pictured at right is Tomas "Tommy" Montoya in 1953, at the then-popular Beachcomber Restaurant in Hollywood. Montoya came to the United States via the U.S. Navy in search of a better life, working his way up from waiter to headwaiter to maitre d' to manager. Montoya's great-grandchildren are now fourth-generation Filipino Angelenos. (Courtesy of Carina Monica Montoya-Forsythe.)

Filipino Americans mingle at a Los Angeles recreational hall in the 1940s. (Courtesy of Carina Monica Montoya-Forsythe.)

Around 1952, a group is gathered on the farm of Mr. Reyes (second from left) in Torrance, near Western Avenue and Artesia Boulevard. Rev. Juan Santos is pictured in the center with Lito Gorospe at far right. Below, another group visits a Torrance farm in the late 1940s. (Above courtesy of Shades of L.A. Archives/ Los Angeles Public Library; below courtesy of Tawa Desuacido.)

Credo Bisquera gets ready to ride his motorcycle in Los Angeles on April 27, 1952. (Courtesy of Shades of L.A. Archives/Los Angeles Public Library.)

The Metro JAC volleyball team included some Filipina American players and is pictured here at the intramural games in February 1954. From left to right are Mae Yamasaki, Alice Fukuda, Natividad Navares, Ami Masushita, Rose Shore, and Lorna Chee. (Courtesy of Shades of L.A. Archives/Los Angeles Public Library.)

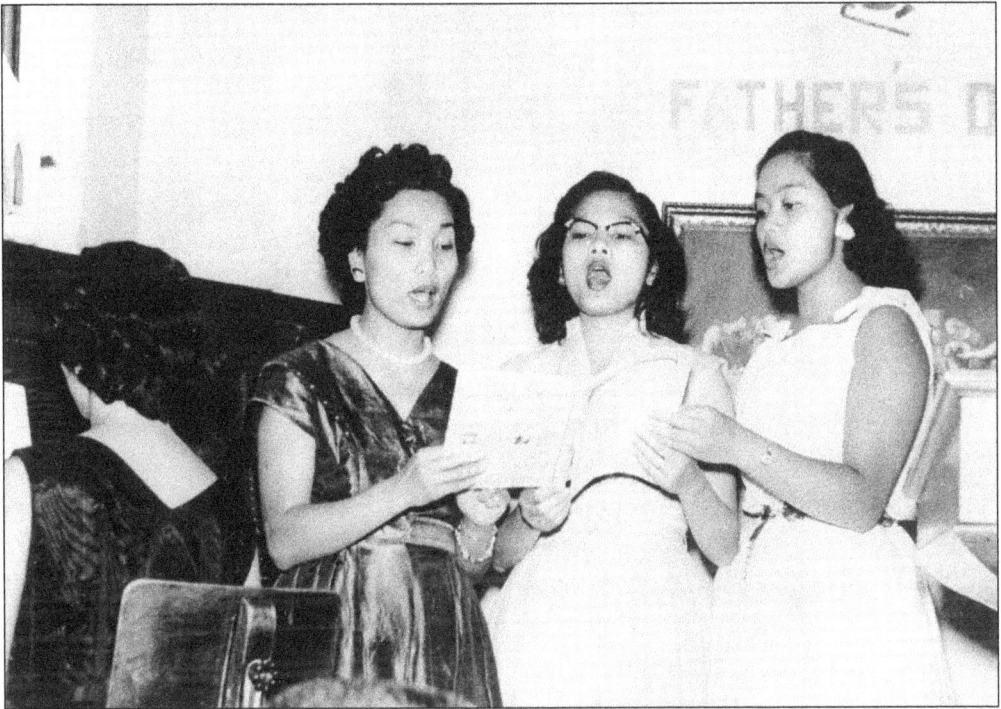

The Filipino Christian Church in Los Angeles holds events for the community throughout the year. Here, some time in the 1950s, members celebrate Father's Day. (Courtesy of Shades of L.A. Archives/Los Angeles Public Library.)

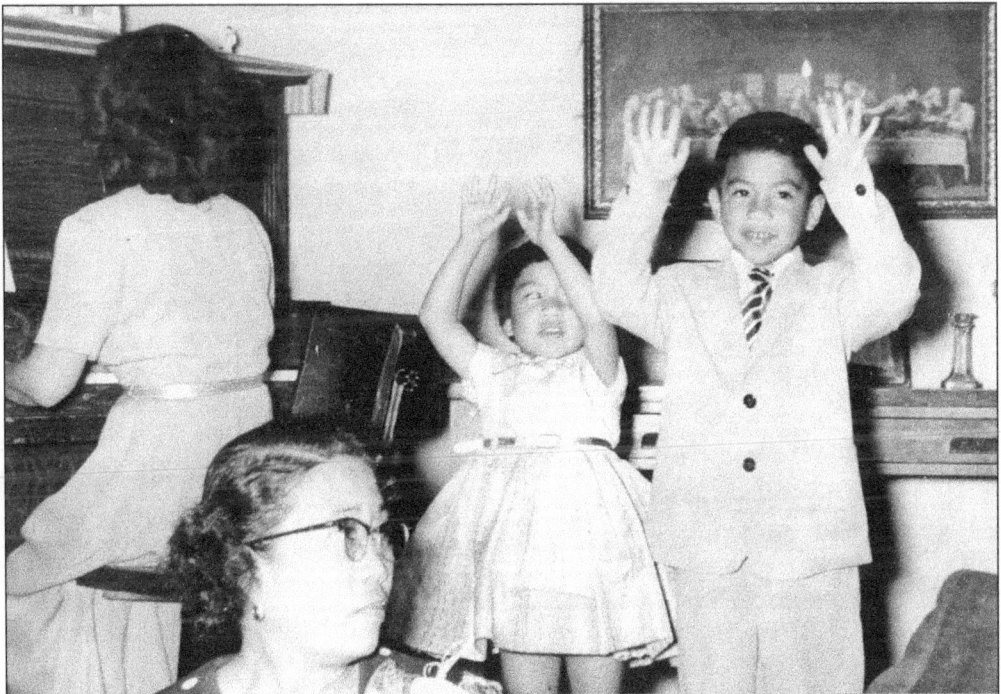

Family and friends celebrate Bruce Palicte's christening at the St. Columban Filipino Catholic Church in Los Angeles on April 21, 1956. From left to right are the baby's father, Joe Palicte; the godfather, Tom Breslin, who is half Irish and half Filipino; Fr. Gerard Byrnes; an unidentified woman holding Bruce; another unidentified woman; Chuck Versola; and the baby's mother, Natividad Palicte. (Courtesy of Shades of L.A. Archives/Los Angeles Public Library.)

On December 24, 1946, an audience gathers for the 20th annual Celebration Christmas Program of the Filipino Federation of America, Inc. (Courtesy of Shades of L.A. Archives/Los Angeles Public Library.)

Rev. Felix Pascua of the Filipino Christian Church sits for a formal photograph with his family in the 1950s. The church, which in 1998 was designated as Historical Cultural Monument No. 651 by the City of Los Angeles Cultural Heritage Commission, is located at 301 North Union Avenue in Los Angeles and is one of the stops of the Historic Filipinotown tours that are currently sponsored by the Filipino American Library. (Courtesy of Hermenia Balderama.)

In 1955, family and friends from the Filipino Christian Church celebrate a baby shower for longtime member Hermenia Balderama, who came to the United States in 1955 and lived in the church parsonage. As a newcomer to America, Balderama said it was the place where she "felt at home." She is seated in the first row, third from the left, and remembers that the church was full every Sunday. (Courtesy of Hermenia Balderama.)

On April 11, 1954, the Holy Name Society gathers at the St. Columban Filipino Catholic Church. (Photograph by Casimiro Obra; courtesy of Benita Q. and Numeriano D. Lagmay.)

Friends and family meet for dinner at the Filipino Christian Church in Los Angeles in 1955. (Courtesy of Shades of L.A. Archives/Los Angeles Public Library.)

Consul and Mrs. Pedro G. Ramirez host a cocktail party in their Los Angeles home in January 1955. (Courtesy of Benita Q. and Numeriano D. Lagmay.)

At a backyard party in Wilmington, Filipino Americans celebrate the christening of Irma Rossi in June 1959. (Photograph by Marcelino Ines Jr.; courtesy of Florante Ibañez.)

In 1957, D. D. Desuacido shows off his catch of the day outside his home in Torrance. (Courtesy of Tawa Desuacido.)

Chris Campos, who immigrated to Hawaii during his teen years, was one of many students recruited to attend Woodbury College in Los Angeles in 1957. Campos became a teacher of business education at St. Paul High School in Santa Fe Springs (located about 14 miles south of downtown Los Angeles) and later taught at the Sawyer College of Business in Pasadena. He fondly remembers those years and recalls that there were "not too many Filipinos" attending Woodbury College. He's proud of the numerous students he's encouraged and taught over the years and says, "I had the American dream." (Courtesy of Chris Campos.)

Three

COMMUNITY LIFE
IN THE 1960S

A surge in Filipino migration to the United States took place after Congress passed the Immigration Act of 1965, which removed national quotas and allowed 170,000 people to immigrate each year from the eastern hemisphere, including as many as 20,000 people from any one country. Filipinos who came to the United States after the law was enacted were part of the third wave of immigrants and, in many cases, came to settle permanently rather than as sojourners. Furthermore, occupational preferences during this time allowed several types of professionals, including nurses and physicians, to qualify for entry into the country. Preference was also given to family members of settled immigrants for reunification, and many *manongs* of the first significant immigrant wave were reunited with their families. The U.S. Census records the Filipino American population of 1960 at 181,614 people. In Los Angeles during the late 1950s, redevelopment of the Bunker Hill area began, and community spaces such as the Filipino American Community of Los Angeles, Inc. (FACLA) and the Filipino Christian Church were replaced by new establishments, including the Dorothy Chandler Pavilion. Displaced Filipino Angelenos relocated farther west into the Temple-Beverly corridor, which today is designated as Historic Filipinotown. They also moved into pockets throughout the city, including some residential areas that once banned minority communities. Pictured here in the 1960s is the ground-breaking ceremony for the new building of FACLA. Today FACLA continues to provide social services to seniors and serves as a venue for community meetings, events, and special occasions. Except where otherwise noted, the majority of photographs in this section are courtesy of Benita Q. Lagmay and her husband, Numeriano D. Lagmay, a professional photographer who immigrated to Los Angeles in 1946. In the 1960s, Lagmay was an active Filipino Angeleno who was often invited to shoot community, church, press, bridal, and family events.

FACLA members and Los Angeles city officials participate in a ribbon-cutting ceremony in the mid-1960s, although the exact event is unknown. The wife of Philippine consul general Alejandro Holigores cuts the ribbon.

The FACLA Building is pictured here at 1740 West Temple Street in today's Historic Filipinotown.

Ben Manibog, president of FACLA
from the early to mid-1960s, shows
a taste of the Philippines to Samuel
William Yorty, the mayor of Los
Angeles from 1961 to 1973, who was
often known as "Mayor Sam."

Community leaders stand in front of Los Angeles City Hall on the Fourth of July in the early to mid-1960s. On the far left is Philippine consul general Alejandro Holigores with an unidentified city official and FACLA president Ben Manibog on the far right.

Former community leader Benita Q. Lagmay recalls the period of the 1960s when each Fourth of July, for Philippine Independence Day, a fund-raiser was held to crown Miss Philippines, with proceeds going back into the community. Typically the coronation took place on the eve of July 4, and the next day consisted of a picnic, followed by a parade that ended at Los Angeles City Hall, where Filipino Angelenos and city leaders made speeches, performed traditional Filipino folk dances, and enjoyed traditional dishes. Here speeches take place at the steps of Los Angeles City Hall downtown just after the parade.

Los Angeles mayor Sam Yorty is pictured with Imelda Marcos (far left) and Ferdinand Marcos (far right), who was the 10th president of the Philippines, from 1965 to 1986, before he was removed from office peacefully by the "People Power" EDSA Revolution. (EDSA is an acronym for Epifanio de los Santos Avenue, which is the main highway in Metro Manila, Philippines, and the site of two peaceful demonstrations that toppled the administration of Philippine presidents Ferdinand Marcos and Joseph Estrada.) Below, the mayor is pictured with Pres. Diosdado Macapagal, the ninth president of the Philippines, from 1961 to 1965.

More FACLA events are pictured here with community and civic leaders, and the American flag hangs with pride in FACLA's main auditorium. (Below courtesy of Jocelyn Geaga-Rosenthal.)

Filipino Angelenos pose for a photograph at the steps in front of Los Angeles City Hall in the 1960s during Philippine Independence Day.

Here community leaders gather at the Consulate General of the Philippines. The Consulate General was established in the 1950s to serve the consular needs of the largest Filipino community outside of the Philippines. It serves as an adjunct of the Philippine government in the overall task of promoting and protecting the national interests of the Philippines and its citizens.

In the 1960s, the Sampaguita Women's Circle (SWC) was active in the Filipino American community of Los Angeles. Here SWC members are photographed at various gatherings. The *sampaguita* flower is the national flower of the Philippines. (Both courtesy of Jocelyn Geaga-Rosenthal.)

Pictured here in the mid-1960s are more gatherings of the Sampaguita Women's Circle. The above photograph takes place at a hotel in downtown Los Angeles. Below, members get ready to serve homemade dishes at a luau buffet. (Above courtesy of Jocelyn Geaga-Rosenthal.)

Seated at the far right during a FACLA event are former U.S. president Ronald Reagan and his wife, Nancy, in the 1960s. In 1966, Reagan was elected governor of California. On the left sits Roque de la Isla with other community members.

Parishioners march in front of the St. Columban Filipino Catholic Church, which had its beginnings in a building on Fedora Street that had served as a Japanese school. Later, in 1946, an old firehouse was converted into a new church building that served the congregation for 20 years. As the parish community continued to grow, another church was built in 1968 at 125 South Loma Street, which still exists today and has an active parish. An ancient Spanish bell recovered from the wartime ruins of the Shrine of Our Lady of Good Voyage in Antipolo, Philippines, is installed in the church's tower.

Filipino Angelenos and friends gather at the Los Angeles home of the Philippine consul general during the 1960s.

This group enjoys a backyard cocktail party during the mid-1960s.

Filipino Angelenos welcome Gemma Cruz (in the feathered hat) to Los Angeles. Cruz was Miss Philippines and went on to be crowned Miss International in 1965, becoming the first Filipina to win the title. The pageant took place in the city of Long Beach.

A Maria Clara Pageant candidate sings at the Statler Hilton Hotel in downtown Los Angeles. The pageant was sponsored by FACLA to raise funds for the Filipino American community. Maria Clara is the heroine of Jose Rizal's book *Noli Me Tangere* and a symbol of the virtues and nobility of the Filipina woman. Rizal is the country's national hero, the most prominent advocate for reforms in the Philippines during the Spanish Colonial era and its eventual independence from Spain.

Members of the Los Angeles Philippines Women's Club and their husbands spend a day at the horse races at Hollywood Park, some time in the 1960s. In the third row from the bottom, seated left to right are Eduard Ramolete, Teo Alemania, two unidentified people, Divinia Alemania, Dolores Ramolete, and Ludi Ongkeko. In the fourth row from the bottom, standing third from the right is Fred Peña. (Courtesy of Shades of L.A. Archives/Los Angeles Public Library.)

Two Filipina Americans pose here for a photograph with their new husbands in the 1960s. In 1933, Filipino Salvador Roldan petitioned for a marriage license to wed Marjorie Rogers, a Caucasian woman. Roldan challenged the anti-miscegenation law in California in the case of *Salvador Roldan v. Los Angeles County* on the basis that Filipinos are of the Malay race and the law originally only banned marriage between Caucasians and "Mongolians, Negroes, Mulattos and persons of mixed blood." Roldan won permission to marry Rogers, but two months later, the Senate amended the anti-miscegenation statute to include the Malay race, and all previous marriages between Filipinos and whites were declared void. Anti-miscegenation laws existed in California until 1948.

A young Filipina wears the traditional American white bridal gown as she prepares for her big day.

An event for the Sampaguita Women's Circle takes place at the Ambassador Hotel in downtown Los Angeles. Pictured at right is Remedios Geaga, who was an active leader in the Filipino American community and former president of FACLA from 1973 to 1975. Below, children dance the *tinikling,* the national dance of the Philippines. The *tinikling* dance mimics the *tikling* birds as they walk between grass stems, run over tree branches, or dodge bamboo traps set by rice farmers. Many children of this generation of FACLA members are those who later helped to originate the tradition of "Pilipino Cultural Night" in Los Angeles County high schools and universities. (Courtesy of Jocelyn Geaga-Rosenthal.)

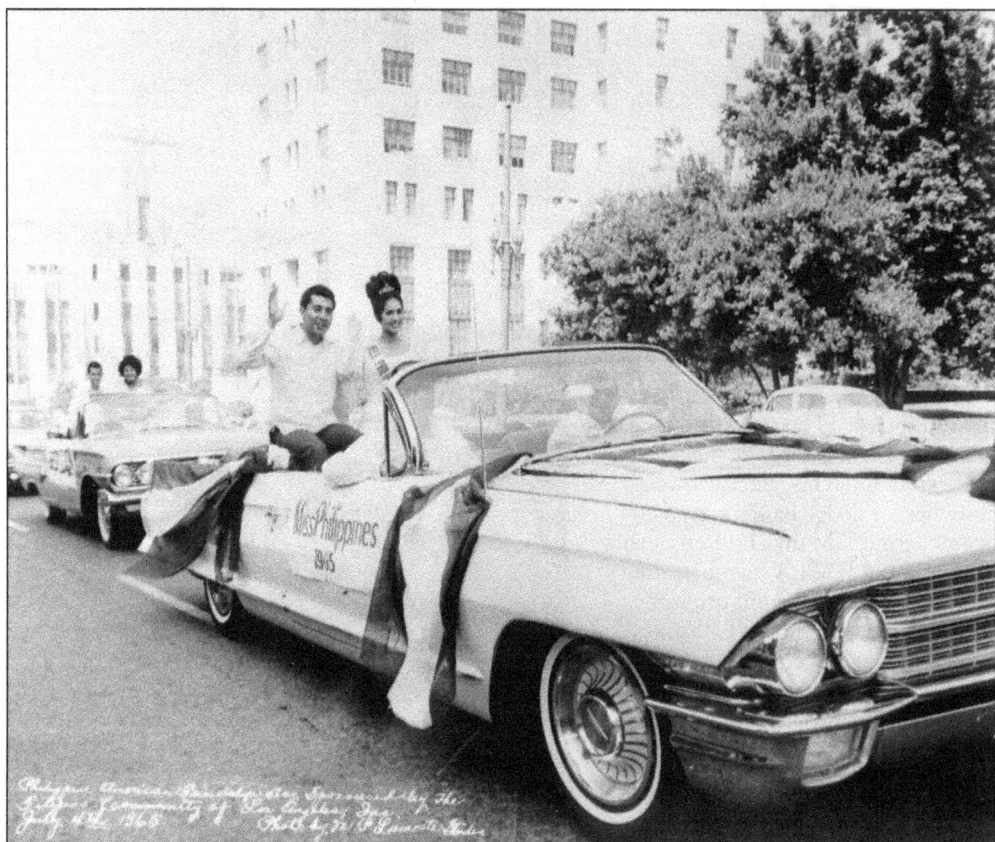

Miss Philippines of FACLA 1965 rides along a downtown street in a Fourth of July parade sponsored by FACLA. The parade was followed by speeches downtown at Los Angeles City Hall. (Courtesy of Shades of L.A. Archives/Los Angeles Public Library.)

Family members, friends, and a proud mother sit with the newly crowned Miss Teenage Philippines, a local pageant sponsored by FACLA.

Pictured here is the winner of the 1968 FACLA Miss Philippines Pageant along with winners from the previous year.

Hundreds of Filipino Angelenos gather at the Hollywood Palladium for a Grand Independence Day Ball and Coronation of the Queen on July 4, 1962, sponsored by the Filipino American Community of Los Angeles, Inc. The Philippine Independence Day event often began with a picnic and

continued with a motorcade to Los Angeles City Hall. At the end of the event was the Coronation of the Queen and the Grand Ball, which lasted well into the evening with music, dancing, family, and friends. (Courtesy of Shades of L.A. Archives/Los Angeles Public Library.)

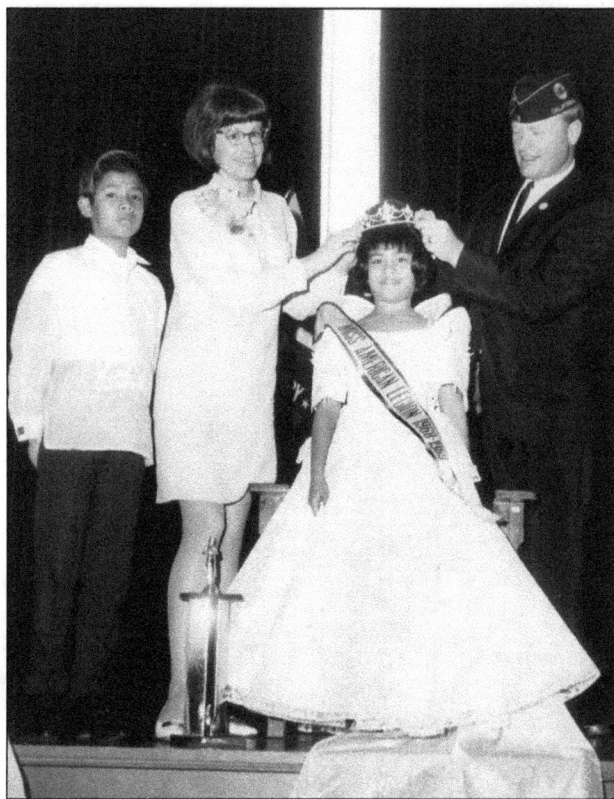

More local community youth pageants from the 1960s are represented here with photographs of Miss American Legion and Miss Sampaguita. Typically any proceeds made from the pageants went back into organizations that benefited the Filipino American community. (Below, courtesy of Jocelyn Geaga-Rosenthal.)

Women of the Los Angeles Philippines Women's Club enjoy a cultural theme night in the mid-1960s, dressing as the Muslim population from the Southern Philippines, known as *Moros*. In the bottom row, fourth from the right is Dolores Ramolete; third from right is Puring Cardenas. In the top row, sixth from right is Elsa Valenzuela. Longtime member Elnora Campos shares that the club was founded in 1961 and also incorporated around that time. The group traditionally attracted professional Filipinas and still exists today. They are listed as one of the original groups in the Founders Circle of the Los Angeles Music Center. (Courtesy of Shades of L.A. Archives/Los Angeles Public Library.)

FACLA presents the first annual Binibni ng Filipinas Debutante Ball at the International Hotel in Los Angeles, on May 30, 1965. Pictured fifth from the right is Jocelyn Geaga-Rosenthal. Today Geaga-Rosenthal, one of the founders of the Historic Filipinotown Improvement Association, is an active community leader and runs a community art gallery called Remy's on Temple, located on Temple Street in Historic Filipinotown. (Courtesy of Jocelyn Geaga-Rosenthal.)

Friends gather to celebrate the birthday of Philippine consul general Alejandro Holigores, pictured here center with his wife, Sofia, to his right.

Neighborhood kids "say cheese" during the birthday of Aniceto Lagmay, who is pictured here in front of his cake. In the back row are Numeriano Leon Lagmay (third from left) and Romeo Lagmay (seated at far right). The house was located on Fifteenth Street at Western Avenue in a diverse ethnic neighborhood, as evidenced by the children who gathered for the party.

Members of the Sampaguita Women's Circle enjoy the comfortable Los Angeles weather during a backyard get-together.

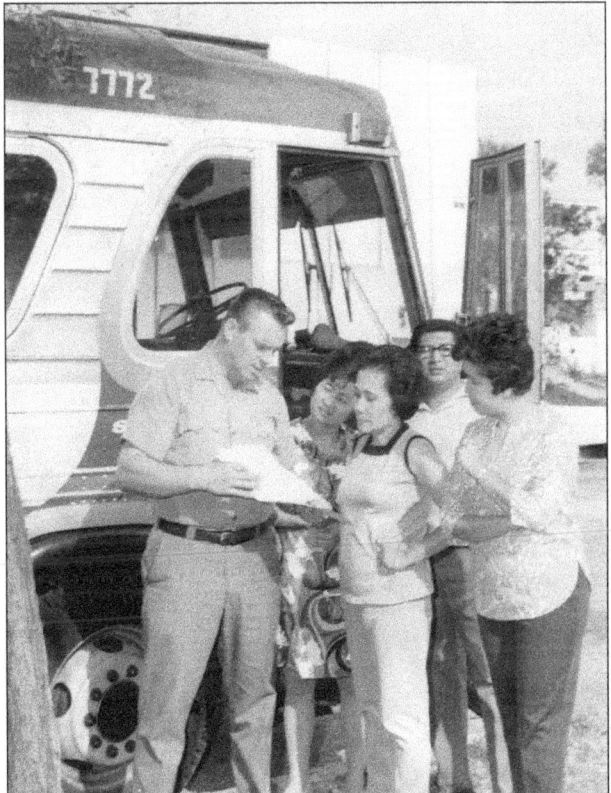

A group of Filipino Angelenos take a bus trip in the 1960s, possibly to Las Vegas. (Courtesy of Jocelyn Geaga-Rosenthal.)

Town mates from Santa Maria, Ilocos Sur, come together in a Los Angeles home in the 1960s. It is commonplace for family and friends who hail from the same provinces and towns in the Philippines to hold gatherings as a way of staying connected to their hometowns.

FACLA members dress up during a Halloween party in the 1960s.

Rudolfo Pulido was one of a large group of Filipino American professionals who immigrated to the United States in the 1960s. This photograph was taken for the Philippine Technical and Professional Society, which was founded in 1961 and consisted of doctors, lawyers, attorneys, and other professionals. Pulido was a civil engineer for the California Division of Highways and worked on such projects as the 405 Freeway. (Courtesy of the Pulido family collection.)

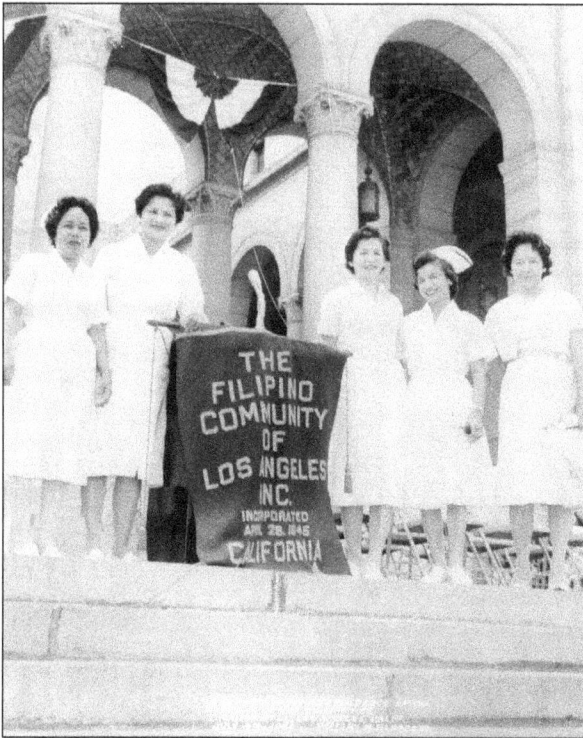

Nurses gather in front of city hall in downtown Los Angeles on July 4, 1961, in celebration of Philippine Independence Day. Dolores Ramolete stands third from the right. (Courtesy of Shades of L.A. Archives/Los Angeles Public Library.)

Mr. and Mrs. Vincent Calzado are pictured here at an American Legion, Manila Post No. 464 event in the 1960s. The gathering took place at Patriotic Hall in Los Angeles.

Four

CHALLENGES, ACHIEVEMENTS, AND EVERYDAY MOMENTS FROM THE 1970S TO TODAY

In the 1970s, Filipino Americans continued to move and establish themselves in various neighborhoods and suburbs throughout Los Angeles County. However, many Filipino Angelenos still moved into the Temple-Beverly corridor—known today as Historic Filipinotown—an area where some families have lived for over 50 years. *Kung may intinanim, may aanihin* is a Tagalog proverb that means, "If you plant a seed and nurture it, you will reap the harvest in the future." Filipino Americans have planted seeds all over the United States. In Los Angeles, they have presence in virtually every aspect of the local community and in social and professional life. They are doctors and nurses, engineers and entertainers, and educators and veterans. They came to this country with nothing and have worked hard to provide a life for their families, passing those values down to their children and grandchildren. They are fifth- and sixth-generation Angelenos. Pictured here on August 17, 1977, a group of *manongs* pass the time by playing cards at the Senior Citizens Club at the FACLA building on Temple Street, located in Historic Filipinotown. (Courtesy of Shades of L.A. Archives/Los Angeles Public Library.)

Filipino groups participate at the Lotus Festival in Echo Park in 1977. The festival was created in 1972 to promote an awareness and understanding of the contributions by the Asian and Pacific Islander communities and is held in July when the lotus flower blooms. Echo Park Lake was chosen as the festival's site as it bears the largest lotus bed in the United States and is conveniently located close to Historic Filipinotown and other Asian communities. (Courtesy of Shades of L.A. Archives/Los Angeles Public Library.)

On June 1, 1977, City of Los Angeles councilmember John Ferraro speaks with Faustino Caigoy, a multidiscipline artist, muralist, and poet whose concerns for the conditions and struggles of his people find expression in his work. This mural was 24 by 54 feet and took Caigoy six months to complete. (Courtesy of Shades of L.A. Archives/Los Angeles Public Library.)

Elderly community members read the newspaper in front of the Filipino American Community of Los Angeles (FACLA) building on Temple Street in Historic Filipinotown. (Courtesy of Photographic Collections, Visual Communications.)

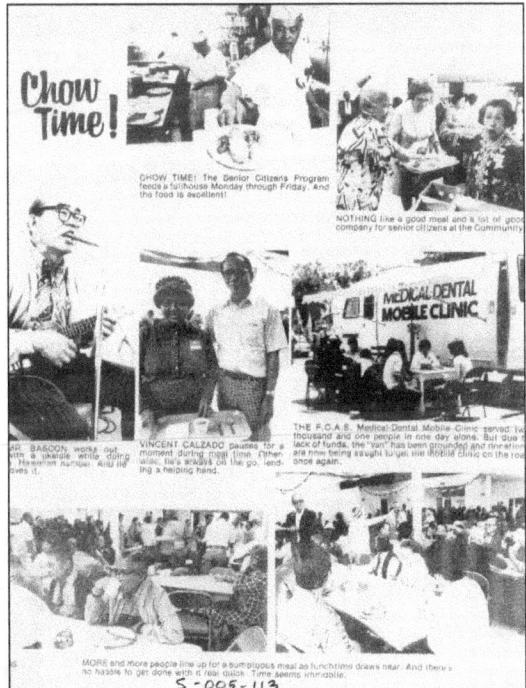

A poster displays various activities and services administered to the Filipino senior-citizen community, c. 1981. (Courtesy of Shades of L.A. Archives/Los Angeles Public Library.)

For over 30 years, Search to Involve Pilipino Americans (SIPA) has served the Historic Filipinotown neighborhood as well as the greater Los Angeles community. SIPA provides health and human services and community economic-development programs to Filipino Americans all over the county. Pictured here is the exterior view of SIPA in the 1970s at their original headquarters. Today the organization is located at 3200 West Temple Street. (Above courtesy of Shades of L.A. Archives/Los Angeles Public Library; below courtesy of Photographic Collections, Visual Communications.)

Royal F. Morales was a community activist, scholar, and social-services leader who taught the popular Pilipino American Experience course at UCLA for nearly two decades before his retirement in 1996. Pictured below, "Uncle Roy" (as he was affectionately known to his students) gives a tour of Historic Filipinotown. Typically, the tour began at the Filipino Christian Church, which Morales's father helped to establish in the 1930s, was followed by a trip to the Pilipino American Reading Room and Library (PARRAL, now known as the Filipino American Library), and then proceeded downtown to the Bunker Hill area, where Filipinos relocated primarily from the early 1940s to the late 1950s. (Above courtesy of Photographic Collections, Visual Communications; below courtesy of the Filipino American Library, Helen Brown Collection.)

A group of youths from the Filipino Christian Church gathers in 1976. Over several years, the church hosted a camp for children and their parents in San Dimas as well as in the San Gabriel Mountains. (Courtesy of Hermenia Balderama.)

SILAYAN

A Philippine Folk Dance Troupe

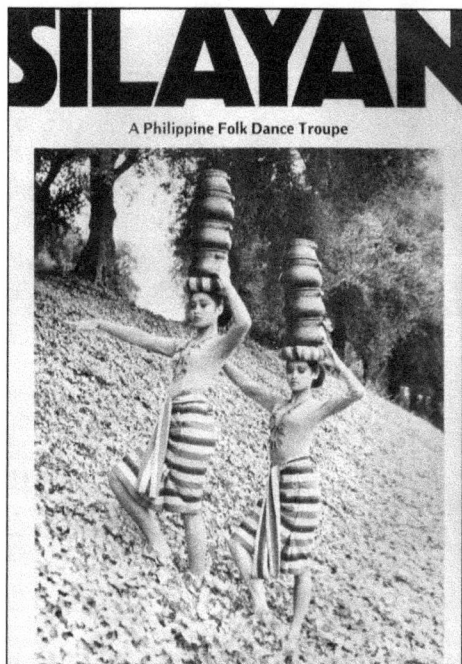

In the early 1970s, Sonia Capadocia, a teacher who immigrated to Los Angeles, taught neighborhood kids from the Temple-Beverly corridor traditional dances in her living room; a few years later, the Silayan Philippine American Dance Company was born. In 1973, the company performed for a sold-out audience in the Dorothy Chandler Pavilion at the Los Angeles Music Center, a milestone for the community in reaching a mainstream audience. Today the multiethnic group is headed by Capadocia's daughter Dulce Capadocia and is the recipient of several awards and grants. They have toured the United States and Europe with an acclaimed repertoire inspired by myths and stories drawn from the human experience and translated into the contemporary American dialogue. (Courtesy of Dulce Capadocia.)

A Filipina American woman
purchases shrimp at a local market.
(Courtesy of the Filipino American
Library, Helen Brown Collection.)

A group of Filipino American
educators and members of the Filipino
American Educators Association,
Inc. (FAEA) are honored in 1988 at a
dinner dance for outstanding teachers
in the Los Angeles Unified School
District (LAUSD), including Lucila
Dypiangco, center. FAEA was founded
in 1974 by Los Angeles teachers and is
affiliated with a statewide association.
Early on, the group served as support
and shelter for teachers who arrived in
the United States. It later evolved into
a professional organization dedicated
to increasing awareness of Filipino
heritage in our schools. Some notable
educators have included Tony Trias
(at lecturn), the first and only Filipino
American member of the LAUSD
School Board, and Carmencita Davino,
a commissioner of the Asian Pacific
Commission in LAUSD. (Courtesy of
Lucila Dypiangco.)

Members of the Philippine Retirees Association gather for their first anniversary in 1984 in the FACLA building in Historic Filipinotown.

This group marches through downtown Los Angeles in 1984 in the Ati-Atihan, a Filipino street parade from the Aklan province of the Philippines, held each January. Celebrants paint their faces with black soot and wear bright costumes as they dance in honor of the Santo Niño. (Courtesy of the Filipino American Library, Helen Brown Collection.)

In the 1970s, more small businesses began to pop up in the Temple-Beverly corridor—today known as Historic Filipinotown—largely as a result of a more professional wave of Filipinos and their families settling in the area. A group called Nayong Pilipinas focused on economic development of Filipino businesses, and they established the Luzon Plaza and other mini-malls. Here people walk toward the plaza with the downtown Los Angeles skyline in the background. (Courtesy of the Filipino American Library, Helen Brown Collection.)

Cesar Lopez shakes hands with former California governor George Duekmejian in 1985. Lopez was the second Filipino honorary mayor of Wilmington, a neighborhood within the city of Los Angeles with a sizeable Filipino American population. He and his wife were the first Filipino couple to own a Denny's restaurant. Like many Filipinos, Lopez taught the value of hard work to his children, including daughter Gina Alexander, a Los Angeles designer whose handbags are sold nationwide and have been featured in *Elle* and *People* magazines, among others. (Courtesy of Gina Alexander.)

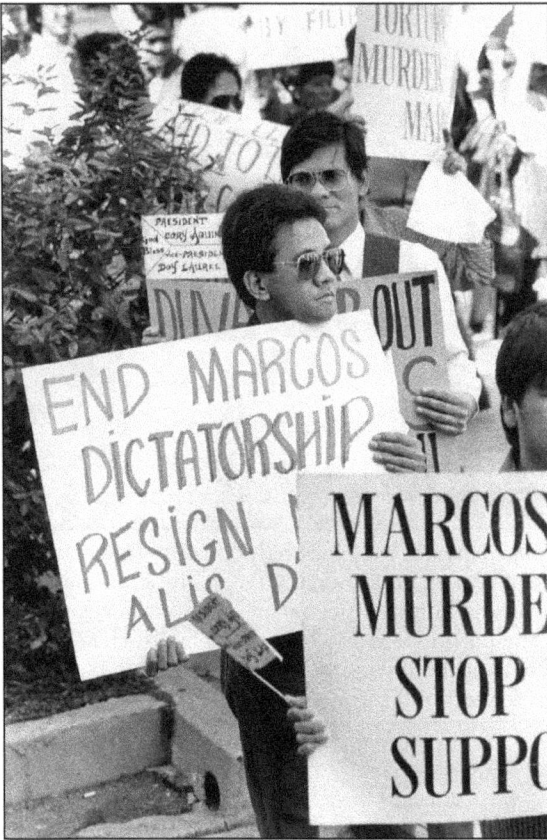

Filipino Americans have long fought for what they believe in. Above, Los Angeles protesters gather to rally against the Marcos regime in the 1980s. Below, people march along Wilshire Boulevard in protest to a visit made by Ferdinand Marcos to Los Angeles in the late 1970s. (Above courtesy of Photographic Collections, Visual Communications; below courtesy of Florante Ibañez.)

Students and community leaders in the 1980s protest the continued presence of U.S. military bases in the Philippines. (Courtesy of the Pulido family.)

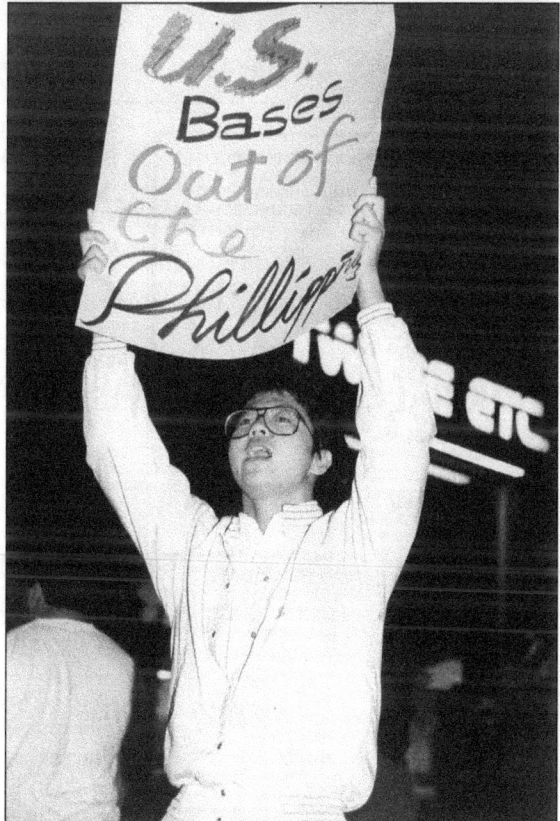

Filipino American quarterback Roman Gabriel played 11 seasons for the Los Angeles Rams, from 1962 to 1972, leading the team to either a first- or second-place finish in their division every year. In 1969, Gabriel was voted the Most Valuable Player of the National Football League for a season in which he threw for 2,549 yards and 24 touchdowns while leading the Rams to the playoffs. (Courtesy of Shades of L.A. Archives/Los Angeles Public Library.)

This poster advertises a contest from Radio Manila in the 1980s. Radio Manila is the first and only Filipino American radio station in the United States that operates 24 hours a day. The station, based in Los Angeles, was established in 1988. (Courtesy of the Filipino American Library.)

NVM Gonzalez (1915–1999), a Filipino writer who was declared Philippines' National Artist for Literature in 1997, speaks at a lecture. The event, which took place at the Philippine Consulate in Los Angeles in the 1980s, was sponsored by the Philippine Expressions Bookshop. (Courtesy of Filipino American Library, Helen Brown Collection.)

The Philippine Expressions Bookshop, the first specialty bookstore in the United States focused primarily on the Philippines, is pictured here in the 1980s at its store on Wilshire Boulevard in Beverly Hills. Today the bookshop is a mail-order store dedicated to Filipino Americans in search of their roots. It creates greater awareness for the literary traditions of the Philippines and the Filipino presence in America by hosting lectures, panels, and author nights. (Courtesy of bookshop owner Linda Nietes.)

Pictured here are participants of the first Southern California Conference of Filipino Immigrant rights, which took place in the late 1970s or early 1980s. Here various organizations and community members came together at the United Methodist Church in Los Angeles to discuss issues affecting the community. One issue of focus was how medical-board testing was conducted in relation to taking cultural considerations into account for nurses and optometrists who had recently emigrated from the Philippines. (Courtesy of Florante Ibañez.)

The identity movement and Third World struggle inspired Asian Americans into political activism and was the framework for establishing Katipunan ng mga Demokratikong Pilipino (KDP), or the Union of Democratic Pilipinos. While the KDP no longer exists, many of its former members remain active in community activities, political organizations, unions, and community-based organizations. Here members of the Los Angeles chapter are pictured during New Year's Eve in the mid-1970s. (Courtesy of Florante Ibañez.)

Gintong Kasaysayan, Gintong Pamana ("A Glorious History, A Golden Legacy") is a 150-foot long mural—half the size of a football field—located along Beverly Boulevard in Historic Filipinotown. The mural, designed in 1995 by artist Eliseo Art Silva, took six months to complete and features portraits of influential Filipinos, largely decided by community input. About his artwork Silva says, "I believe that love within our hearts engages our minds in order to activate the hands and create works of art—transforming passive subjects to active citizens. Thus, the mural itself is a container of love in the hope that this love will engage our community to reconcile western structure/body with Filipino substance/soul." The mural aims to tell the Filipino story of migration and transformation, awakening memories of the land while at the same time evoking the rich stories and experiences brought into the surrounding neighborhood by Filipino Americans. Above is the wall before the mural was painted. Below, Silva stands at right with Filipino artist, playwright, and activist Timoteo Cordova. (Courtesy of Eliseo Art Silva)

Francisco "Tony" Respicio Jr. visits the 1984 Olympics, held in Los Angeles. Respicio settled in Los Angeles just 10 years prior and established his home in West Covina. The eldest of nine siblings, his father, Franky T. Respicio, was a prisoner of war and survivor of the Bataan Death March. Many Filipino families continued to migrate to Southern California suburbs throughout the 1970s and 1980s. (Courtesy of Jennifer Respicio.)

The World Kulintang Institute and Research Studies Center, Inc., is dedicated to the preservation, education, and presentation of the rare, centuries-old, traditional, gong-and-drum ensemble music from the Southern Philippines. Currently the organization, whose members are pictured here during a performance, is located in the San Fernando Valley of Reseda. (Courtesy of the Pulido family collection.)

Pilipino Cultural Night, best known as PCN, is an event where students share their culture on stage through song, stories, and traditional folk dances and takes place at high schools and colleges across the country. Pictured above around 1984 is the PCN from Club Kaibigan of Whitney High School—one of the first high schools to hold a PCN in the Los Angeles County area. (Courtesy of the Pulido family collection.)

Pictured here is the figure representing the Philippines in the Disneyland ride "It's a Small World." Disneyland is one of the most well-known Los Angeles landmarks. (Courtesy of the Pulido family collection.)

In 1992–1993, Mark Pulido served as the first Filipino American undergraduate student-body president at the University of California, Los Angeles. Other student-body presidents of Los Angeles universities have included Jenny Punsalan Wood of UCLA (2005–2006) and Kristina Alagar and Holly Rana Lim of the University of California, Riverside. (Courtesy of the Pulido family collection.)

Students of the University of California, Irvine celebrate "Pilipino graduation," popularly known as "P-grad." Various Filipino American student organizations in Los Angeles include Kaibigans at Cal State Fullerton, Today's Organization of Pilipinos at Long Beach City College, Isang Bansa at Loyola Marymount University, Filipino American Student Association at Cal State Northridge, the Filipino American Student Organization at Pasadena City College, Hiyas Club at Cal State Los Angeles, Samahang Pilipino at UCLA, Katipunan at UC Riverside, and Troy Philippines at USC. These groups all work to inform students and the community about Filipino culture and to provide a support network for Filipino American students. (Courtesy of Florante Ibañez.)

Pictured here the day after the Los Angeles riots is the Goldilocks Bakery, located on Vermont Avenue in Los Angeles. Students and community members came together to assist in cleaning up during the aftermath. (Courtesy of the Pulido family collection.)

Filipino Americans—such as Perry Barrit, who ran for Cerritos City Council—have long been involved in city politics. Over the years, other Filipino American officials within the County of Los Angeles have included City of Carson mayor Peter Fajardo; City of Carson councilmembers Lorelie Olaes, Manny Ontal, and Elito Santarina; City of Duarte councilmember Tzietl Paras; City of Vernon councilman William Davis; and mayor pro tem for the City of Walnut Tony Cartegena. (Courtesy of the Pulido family collection.)

Students practice at Dance Village, a dance school owned by Ed Coscolluella, pictured at far right, in Eagle Rock. (Photograph by and courtesy of Shatto Light.)

The *Flores de Mayo* (Flowers of May) is a yearly festival celebrated by Filipino Catholics in which youths wearing white offer flowers to the Virgin Mary. Here the festival concludes with a traditional march and pageant called the *Santa Cruzan*. (Courtesy of the Pulido family collection.)

102

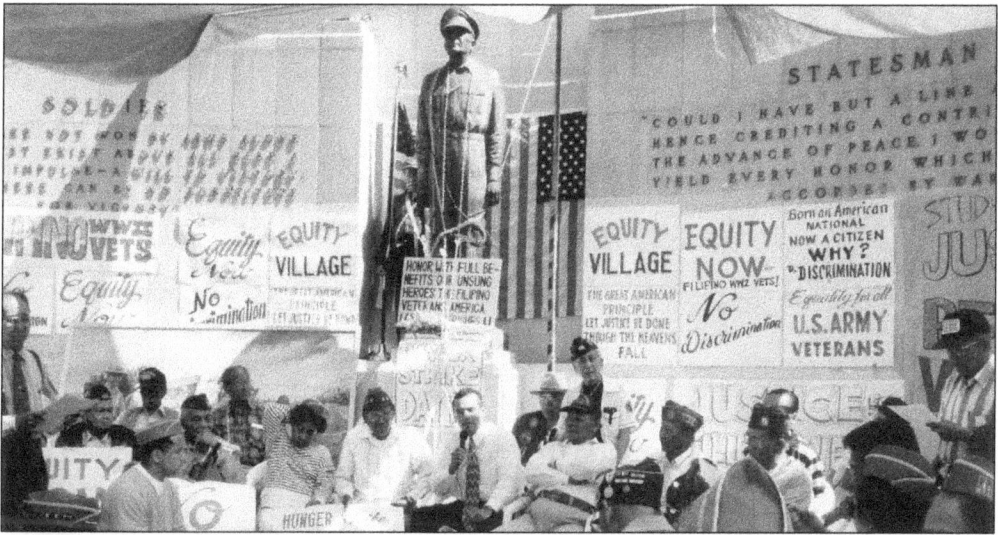

In 1997, Filipino American veterans established an "Equity Village" at MacArthur Park in Los Angeles, named after their former commander in chief. Fifty veterans participated in a hunger strike and took turns being chained while fighting for a bill that would amend the Recission Act of 1946, which denied rights and benefits to members of the Philippines Commonwealth Army because their activities were not considered active service under the U.S. Armed Forces. An event flier read, "[The veterans] have waited long enough to be given the recognition of their invaluable service to the United States of America so that we may be free . . . They did not question America when they were young fighting men." Pictured at center is councilman Antonio Villaraigosa, the current mayor of Los Angeles. (Courtesy of the Pulido family collection.)

Today Filipino American Veterans continue their fight for equal rights. Here at the 2002 Justice for Filipino Veteran's Rally, children shout in support. Loralei Rose Bingamon, a multiracial, second-generation *Pinay* says, "Knowing the *manongs* continued to die without ever being recognized by the United States—sadness was a part of me at the march. However, seeing young and old side-by-side and witnessing the strength of the Filipino community, I left with a sense of empowerment and pride." (Courtesy of Loralei Rose Bingamon.)

SLAIN POSTMAN TO BE BURIED TODAY

Asians decry rising tide of hate

Bishops rebuff Erap on Charter change

MANILA--Catholic bishops on Thursday met for lunch with President Estrada in Malacañang, but emerged unconvinced that the Constitution should be amended at this time.

In an interview with reporters later, three of the four bishops present at the meeting said the Aug. 20 rally to be led by former President Corazon Aquino and Jaime Cardinal Sin in Makati City would push through.

But the President himself described the meeting to reporters as "very, very fruitful."

Asked if it could be called a success, he said: "I believe

He added: "I answered all the issues, explained all the issues to them, and the advice of (Manila Auxiliary) Bishop (Teodoro) Bacani is to disseminate all this information regarding the Concord, the Charter change, (wherein) we are only interested in economic reforms."

Asked if the bishops kept an "open mind" during the meeting which lasted almost three hours, Mr. Estrada

See BISHOPS on Page 14

This time, the press is the core of news

By MAX G. ALVAREZ

(The author recently wrapped up a two-week Philippine story assignment. The following segment focuses on the media and the unique position of newspersons in the Philippine social milieu.)

MANILA, Philippines--As the capital city of the Philippines, Manila holds some kind of distinction as the veritable cradle of newspapers.

There must at least be more than 20 daily publications in this city, counting all the broadsheets and the tabloids.

The figure beats the record of Los Angeles, which is known for its lone Los Angeles Times and, partly in L.A. and largely in the San Fernando Valley, for the success of the Daily News. Surrounding cities of L.A. of course boast of such noted publications as the Orange County Register, the Long

See PRESS on Page 19

THE Asian Pacific American community on Friday joined the Jewish and other communities to decry the rising tide of hate as another Asian Pacific American victim, Joseph Ileto, fell victim to a hate shooting.

Asian Pacific American Legal Center executive director Stewart Kwoh, in a press statement said: "Hate crimes affect everyone, not just the victims, their community or their family. We should join together with communities across the nation, of all backgrounds, to deplore and bring an end to these kinds of attacks."

He also said, "Congress must delay no more in passing the Hate Crimes Prevention Act."

The Hate Crimes Prevention Act passed the Senate, but is currently stalled in the House of Representatives Judiciary Committee. The Act, he added, will help states to combat hate crimes, analyze data collected to assess states' performance in prosecuting hate crimes, and allow federal prosecution of hate crimes committed across multiple state lines.

Susan Maquindang, executive director of the Filipino American Service Group Inc., said, "hate

See ASIANS on Page 16

RELATIVES of victims believed buried under the debris of collapsed houses of Cherry Hills subdivision in Antipolo City wait patiently for the results of the ongoing retrieval operations. (SNSwirephoto)

Agriculture posts 6.76% growth in 1st half of 1999

MANILA--The Department of Agriculture (DA) ruled out yesterday any possible rice importation this year, saying that the country has sufficient supply of this basic commodity as it disclosed a 6.76 percent growth in agricultural production for the first semester of 1999.

"The farm sector's performance from January to June this year is good," Angara said, "with corn leading the list of the farm produce, which provided the nation with a relatively impressing performance of 103.12 percent followed by palay crops with 48.13 percent."

The livestock industry gave a slight improvement in its performance with a total growth of 5.80 percent while the fishery sector's growth was placed at 1.18 percent, Angara said.

Latest inventory of rice showed that the country has 144 days supply of this commodity, which would last until the end of this year, he said.

Of the total rice stock, the National Food Authority (NFA) has
See AGRICULTURE on Page 18

Developer had mining permit on Cherry Hills

MANILA--The Philippine-Japan Solidarity Corp. (Philjas) has been given a permit to mine from 1994 to 1996 portions of the mountain near the Cherry Hills Subdivision in Antipolo City, site of the
See CHERRY on Page 16

PHILIPPINE National Police (PNP) acting chief Director General Edmundo Larroza (left) and Chief Supt. Jewel Canson (right) inspects the 28 kilos of shabu worth P56 million pesos seized from suspected big-time drug trafficker Jimmy Shi alias Henry Chua (center) after the raid conducted by the combined elements from the Presidential Anti-Organized Crime Task Force (PAOCTF) and Narcotics Group at the shabu warehouse in Quezon City. (SNSwirephoto)

Along with the *Asian Journal*, *California Examiner*, and other organizations, Balita Media, Inc., has been informing the Filipino American community in Southern California since 1991. This particular headline focuses on Joseph Ileto, a Filipino American postman from Whittier (a Los Angeles suburb) who in 1999 was gunned down in a hate-related shooting. The Ileto family has since become national spokespersons for awareness of hate crimes and gun control. (Courtesy of Balita Media, Inc.)

Founded in the early 1990s, the mission of the Filipino American National Historical Society is to "promote understanding, education, enlightenment, appreciation, and enrichment through the identification, gathering, preservation, and dissemination of the history and culture of Filipino Americans in the United States." Here, c. 1995, members of the Los Angeles chapter (FANHS-LA) hold a strategic planning retreat at the Japanese American Community Cultural Center in Los Angeles. Pictured here are Meg Malpaya Thornton (far left), Phil Ventura (third from left), Darline Ventura, August Espiritu, Bruce Palicte, and Joe Palicte. (Courtesy of the Filipino American Library.)

Papo de Asis, a Philippine-born artist known worldwide for his art, has created socially conscious artwork since the 1970s. De Asis led workshops and contributed numerous murals and banners for demonstrations, conferences, and political forums. He cofounded with Melissa Roxas and Jenn True the organization Habi Ng Kalinangan (also known as Habi Arts), a collective of Los Angeles artists committed to political and artistic empowerment for progressive social change. (Photograph by and courtesy of Apollo Victoria.)

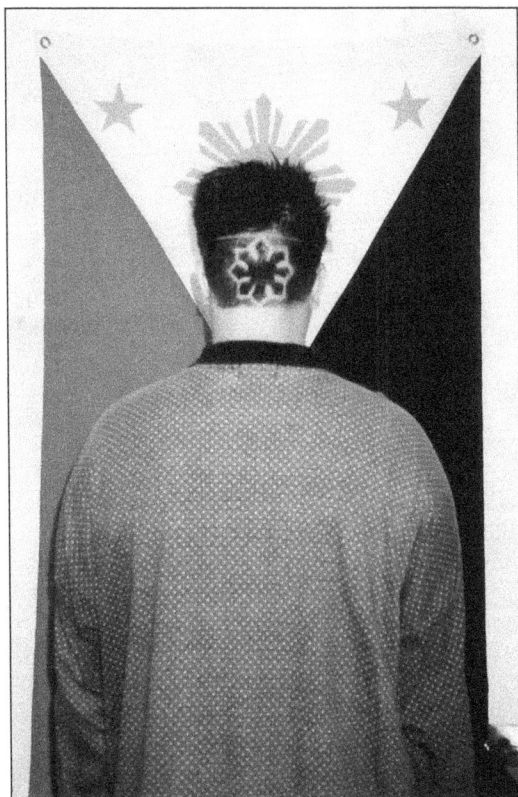

Around 1990, Ariel Mercado shows his cultural pride and spirit in a unique way. Mercado is a second-generation *Pinoy* whose parents came to the United States in the third wave of immigrant professionals. (Courtesy of the Pulido family collection.)

Filipino American performers sing onstage during the 2006 Festival of Philippine Arts and Culture, held at Point Fermin Park in San Pedro. (Courtesy of Florante Ibañez.)

The Festival of Philippine Arts and Culture (FPAC) first took place at Los Angeles City College on Mother's Day in 1992, the week after the L.A. riots. Even in the aftermath, 3,000 participants attended. Today it is the largest presenter of Philippine arts and culture in Southern California, attracting over 20,000 attendees nationwide and featuring over 1,200 artists. FPAC, first organized by approximately 100 artists and community leaders, is still a community-led effort produced by a core group of volunteer professionals in collaboration with community and civic organizations and hundreds of volunteers. Pictured here are moments from FPAC's earliest years. (Courtesy of FilAm ARTS.)

Los Angeles is home to a rich literary community. Here Filipino American author Noel Alumit signs his novel *Letters to Montgomery Clift* at a reading at Skylight Books in the Los Angeles neighborhood of Los Feliz. Alumit's book follows a young Filipino boy sent to America by his parents to escape the brutal Marcos regime. It is a story of hope set against a backdrop of abuse and alienation. (Courtesy of Noel Alumit.)

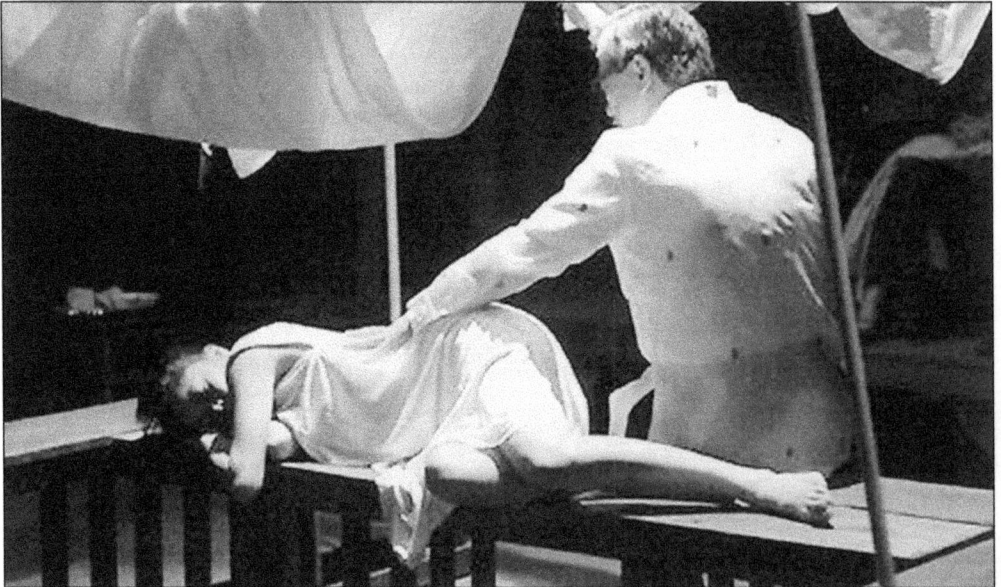

In 2004, the Search to Involve Pilipino Americans (SIPA) organization, in association with the Playwrights' Arena, produced *Dogeaters*, which appeared at the new SIPA Performance Space in Los Angeles. The play was author Jessica Hagedorn's stage adaptation of her 1990 best-selling and National Book Award nominated novel. Here is a scene from the play with Esperanza Catubig (lying down), who plays Miss Philippines, and Dana Lee. (Photograph by Michael Anthony Hermoge; courtesy of the play's director, Jon Lawrence Rivera.)

Imelda: A New Musical premiered at the East West Players in 2005, the country's premier Asian American theatre. The musical biography was performed by an all Asian American cast, and the production went on to become the theatre's second highest selling show in their 40-year history. From left to right are Antoine Reynaldo Diel as Benigno "Ninoy" Aquino, Myra Cris Ocenar as Corazon "Cory" Aquino, Liza Del Mundo as Imelda Marcos, and Giovanni Ortega as Ferdinand Marcos. (Photograph by Michael Lamont; courtesy of East West Players' Archives.)

Many Filipino artists' studios and galleries were featured in a 2006 Open Studio Tour, including Rod Samonte, whose artwork is featured in the background during a reception at the Brand Library in Glendale. At the far left is Zen Lopez, the first Filipina American to be appointed as Arts and Culture Commissioner for the City of Glendale. (Photograph by and courtesy of Vics Magsaysay.)

On the set of the Showtime series *Barbershop*, Sydney Shiotani, a second-generation Filipino, got to call out: "Quiet on the set—we're rolling!" Her mother, Jennifer Aquino Shiotani, has appeared on stage and screen, including in a 2004 *Without a Trace* television episode in which the character was written specifically for a Filipina American actress. Filipinos throughout Los Angeles continue to appear in front of the camera and work in all capacities of the development and production of projects for stage, television, and film. (Courtesy of Jennifer Aquino Shiotani.)

Apl.de.Ap, part of the Grammy Award–winning group Black Eyed Peas, is pictured here in a scene from the video *Bebot (Generation One)*, directed by second-generation "indie" filmmaker Patricio Ginelsa. About his craft Ginelsa says, "Why is it that I can count all the films depicting the Filipino American experience in less than 10 fingers? That's what motivates me as a filmmaker. I feel it's one of my responsibilities to represent those who don't have a voice in the mainstream. You can't expect Hollywood to tell your stories for you. I take pride in not only creating these projects, but educating people in the community about the importance of media representation and supporting films about the community." (Photograph by SthanLee B. Mirador; courtesy of Patricio Ginelsa.)

Pictured here is a scene from *Brown Soup Thing*, a comedic film about four generations of Filipinos struggling to get along in America. Edward J. Mallillin, the film's director and producer, says, "One thing I found very inspiring about the movie was so many of the actors enjoyed getting back in touch with their heritage. I got the sense that being a Filipino was/is important to everyone involved and this was a unique opportunity for so many of us to merge our personal interests and professional goals into one thing." From left to right are actresses Cheryl Noe, Sari Arambulo, and Kimee J. Balmilero. (Photograph by Svetlana Dekic; courtesy of Malinius.)

Ruben Aqunio is an award-winning veteran artist for Walt Disney Feature Animation, having worked as a supervising animator on such animated classics as *The Little Mermaid*, *The Lion King*, *Beauty and the Beast*, *Pocahontas*, and *Mulan*. (Courtesy of Walt Disney Feature Animation and Ruben Aquino.)

Across the country, many town mates form organizations in the United States to stay connected. Members from the village of Calayab in the town of Santo Domingo, located in the province of Ilocos Sur, meet here during the late 1980s or early 1990s at a Los Angeles hotel for their annual Sons and Daughters of Santo Domingo dinner and dance. (Courtesy of Jennifer Respicio.)

In 2001, family members enjoyed a "Zamora Clan Reunion" in West Covina, an annual event that started in the Philippines in the 1970s and continued in the United States in the 1980s, as more family members continued to move to the United States. Large reunions are common for Filipino Americans, reflecting the Filipino-held value of faithfulness to the family. (Courtesy of Rona Par.)

At this debutante ball (popularly called a debut), a young Filipina celebrates her 18th birthday. Lara Andrea Avengoza dances with her cotillion court, nine boys and nine girls, in an elegant waltz. Other traditions include the debutante dancing with 18 boys, each one offering her a rose, and 18 young ladies lighting 18 candles to serve as guidance to the debutante during her transition into womanhood. (Photograph by and courtesy of Shatto Light.)

The Kiwanis Club of Fil-Am Glendale presented the Children Helping Children Fashion Show at the Glendale Civic Auditorium in May 2006 in partnership with the Glendale Unified School District. The event benefited schoolchildren with special needs and was emceed by KABC-TV Channel 7 anchorwoman Denise Dador, a Filipina American. (Photograph by and courtesy of Vics Magsaysay.)

Community members perform at an event for the Filipino American Service Group, Inc. (FASGI) in the mid-1980s. Established in 1981, FASGI serves the needy of downtown Los Angeles and provides food and nutrition services, client advocacy, care management, and emergency- and transitional-housing services to such areas as Central Los Angeles, Echo Park, Silver Lake, Hollywood, and Historic Filipinotown. (Courtesy of the Filipino American Library, Helen Brown Collection.)

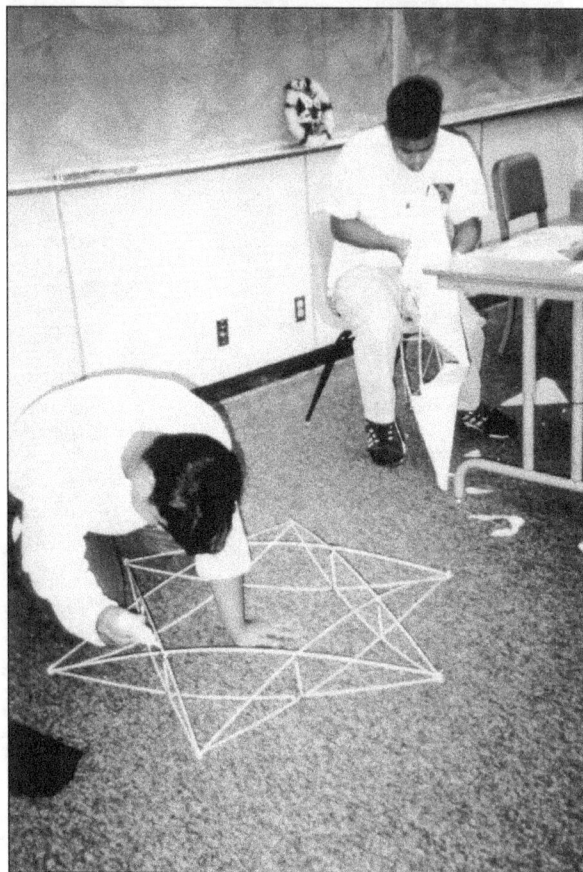

In 1994, at Cerritos College, students learn how to make a Philippine *parol* (Christmas lantern). *Parols* have a bamboo frame and are covered with colored tissue paper. They are commonly used to decorate Filipino households during Christmastime. (Courtesy of Shades of L.A. Archives/Los Angeles Public Library.)

Members of the Kultura Philippine Folk Arts Dance Company are pictured here performing traditional dances. Above, young girls dance the *sakuting*, which originated from the province of Abra and interprets a mock fight between the Ilokano Christians and non-Christians. This dance is traditionally performed during Christmas in town plazas or from home to home, where, in exchange for the dance, the dancers receive *aguinaldo*—presents, money, or refreshments. Below is a dance called *binasuan*, which means "with the use of drinking glasses." It originated from the Pangasinan Province and is commonly performed during weddings, fiestas, and other special occasions. Glasses are filled with rice wine and dancers gracefully move with the glasses placed on their heads and hands. (Courtesy Balita Media, Inc.)

In 1966, the Goldilocks story began when two sisters and their sister-in-law opened a small bakeshop in Makati, Philippines. Years later, the shop has become a Filipino icon, serving baked goods and traditional dishes in the Philippines, the United States, and Canada. In 1976, Goldilocks opened their first Los Angeles store in Artesia, and bakeshops can now be found in L.A., Cerritos, Eagle Rock, Panorama City, and West Covina. Mary-Ann Ortiz-Luis, president of Clarmil Manufacturing, the manufacturing arm of Goldilocks, says, "We wanted the Filipinos of Southern California to have a taste of great food as we know it in the Philippines, to remind them of things they grew up with." (Courtesy of Goldilocks.)

Remy's on Temple is an art gallery located at 2126 West Temple Street in Historic Filipinotown. It showcases work by Filipino Americans and hosts readings, exhibits, and other community events. Founded as a celebration of the legacy of former community leader Remedios V. Geaga, the gallery is owned by her daughter Jocelyn Geaga-Rosenthal. Here Doris Magsaysay, a retired educator, visits an art exhibition. The work of professional photographer and artist Vics Magsaysay hangs behind her. Geaga says, "I think young people know there's a hunger for learning what their roots are." (Courtesy of Vics Magsaysay.)

116

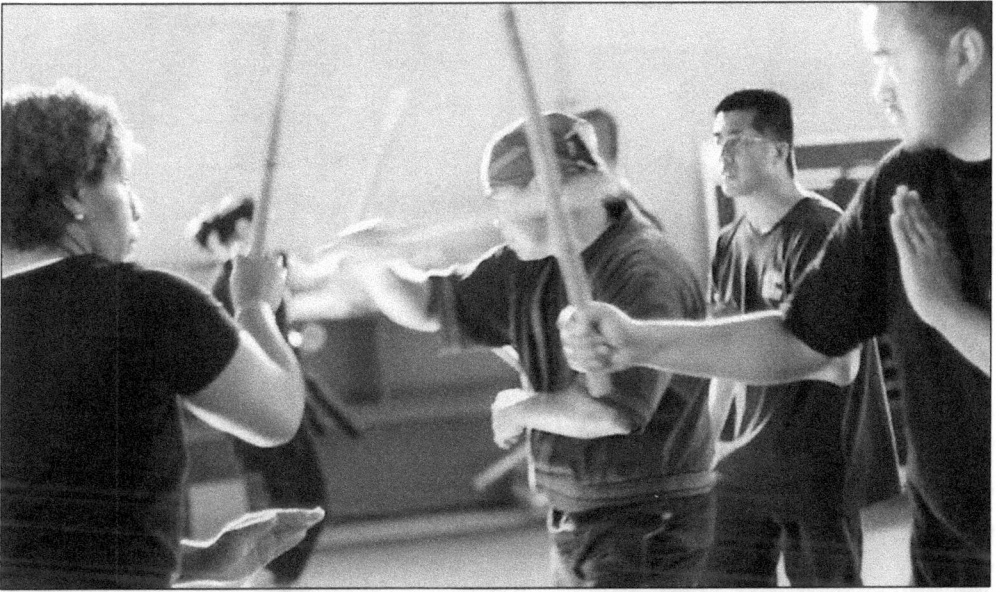

Students from the Kali Klub sa FilAm ARTS practice the art of *Lameco Eskrima*. Kali Klub is a project of *Kapisanang Mandirigma*, which started as a positive diversion against drugs and gangs for youths. Now in their ninth year, they teach youths, adults, and elders the warrior arts of the Philippines in a noncommercial, nonpolitical, combat-realistic environment where art, culture, and heritage are integrated into the curriculum. From left to right are students Teshima Walker and Cheryl Samson, instructor Arnold A. Noche (center), and students Manuel Paglinawan and Joseph Bernardo. (Courtesy of Arnold A. Noche.)

A Filipina American performs at a 2006 meeting of the San Fernando Valley Filipino American Chamber of Commerce. (Photograph by and courtesy of Karlo David.)

At age 83, Lourdes "Lulu" Astilla became the first female elected as commander of the Filipino Veteran's Association, an affiliate of the Filipino Veteran's Foundation of Los Angeles. Lulu, whose husband was a World War II veteran, came to the United States in 1981; she is the great-grandmother of three. She says, "I am very happy I am here in the U.S. and still able to help people." She is pictured here (center) dancing at a United Nation's Day celebration in the San Gabriel Adult Day Health Care Center. (Courtesy of Lulu Astilla.)

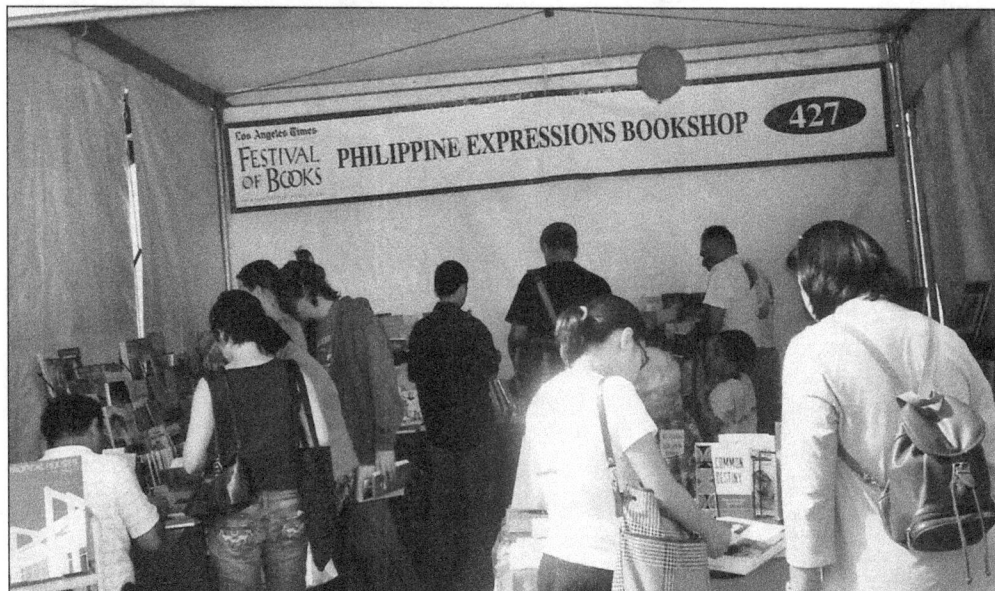

The Philippine Expressions Bookstore displays an array of books focused on the Filipino culture at the *Los Angeles Times* Festival of Books, one of the country's largest literary events. It draws over 130,000 attendees from across the United States. (Courtesy of Linda Nietes.)

Filipina American actress Tia Carerra sings at the Filipino American Library's Sixth Annual Spirit Awards and Gala. The awards acknowledge the important contributions that individuals and organizations have made to the Filipino American community, and proceeds benefit the library's collection, public programming, and outreach efforts. Past honorees have included such individuals as Hollywood producer Dean Devlin; Stewart Kwoh, executive director of the Southern California Asian Pacific American Legal Center; actor Lou Diamond Phillips, and Lisa Yuchengco, founder of *Filipinas Magazine*. (Photograph by Karlo David; courtesy of the Filipino American Library.)

The Filipino American Library (FAL) is committed to its mission of serving as a primary educational and cultural resource for the community. Their programming has included research projects, film screenings, play readings, art exhibits, and public lectures and workshops on law, entertainment, government, and health. The library is located in Historic Filipinotown in the same building as the Filipino American Service Group, Inc. (FASGI). Pictured here in 2006, people enjoy the library's offerings. (Photograph by Karlo David; courtesy of Filipino American Library.)

Angelenos continue to fight for equal rights for Filipino American Veterans, pictured here during a recent Justice for Filipino American Veteran's Day parade in Historic Filipinotown. On Veterans Day 2006, a memorial of five large, black, granite monoliths engraved with photographs and text of veterans' stories was dedicated in Lake Street Park to honor the brave Filipinos who fought side-by-side with American soldiers during World War II. In 1990, a federal law was passed awarding citizenship to Filipinos who had fought on the side of the United States during World War II. The legislation, however, did not consider veteran's benefits. In commemoration of the 60th anniversary of the fall of Bataan, Pres. George W. Bush and the U.S. Congress are being asked to support new legislation that would extend full and equitable benefits to the veterans. The memorial makes a statement of support for these efforts. (Courtesy of Balita Media, Inc.)

Filipino comedian and performer Rex Navarette took the stage as one of the Philippine Festival of Arts and Culture's main headliners in 2006, which marked the event's 15th year. It was attended by 20,000 people. (Photograph by Ernie Peña; courtesy of FilAm ARTS.)

In 2004, Oscar Azarcon Solis, a Roman Catholic priest born in the Philippines, was ordained at the Cathedral of Our Lady of the Angels as one of five auxiliary bishops in the Archdiocese of Los Angeles, named by Pope John Paul II to head the archdiocese's coordinating council focusing on minority issues. Three thousand people, including 700 priests, packed the cathedral where, during part of the procession, Filipino Americans in native costumes danced the *pandango sa ilaw*. Bishop Solis told the press, "I consider my appointment more than just an opportunity to become a part of the local church of Los Angeles, but more as a distinct privilege to serve our archdiocese, which is alive and vibrant with multiethnic communities." (Courtesy of Balita Media, Inc.)

In July 2006, for the second time since 1994, the Los Angeles Dodgers invited Willie Gaa, the Philippine consul general of Los Angeles, to throw the ceremonial pitch for "Filipino American Community Night" before one of their games. The Sining Kambayoka Group, a nonprofit cultural organization with a mission of promoting Filipino culture and heritage, performed the *singkil* dance, and the Philippine national anthem was sung for an audience of thousands. (Courtesy of Balita Media, Inc.)

The Filipino and American flags fly in front of the Los Angeles consul general's home in Hancock Park to commemorate Philippine Independence Day. (Courtesy of Balita Media, Inc.)

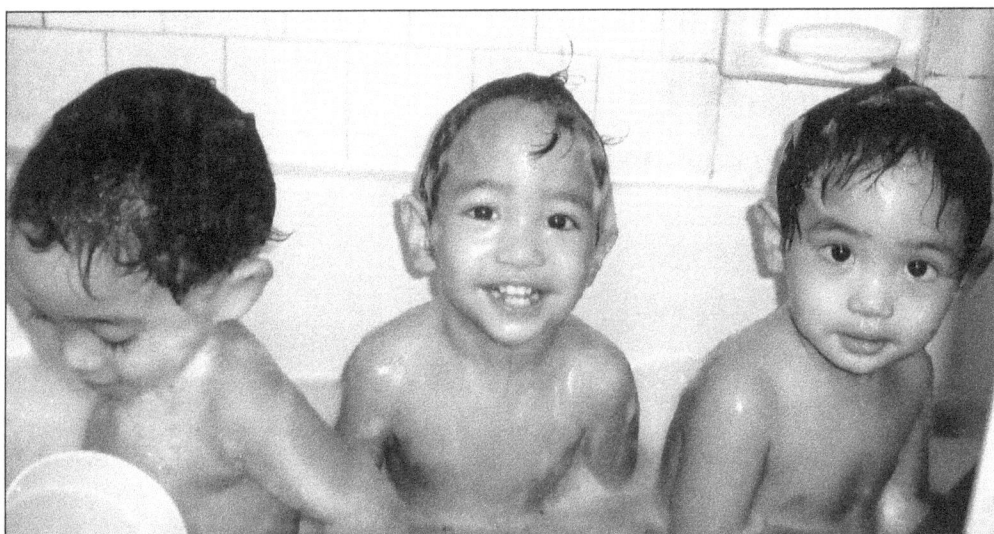

A Los Angeles native and second-generation Filipino, Ron Albino is finishing school and working full-time while his family helps him raise triplet boys. Albino finds strength in the family unit and refers to his mother's favorite saying: "There is no difficulty that enough love can't conquer." Enjoying a bath from left to right are Josef, Julian, and Jonathan. (Courtesy of Ron Albino.)

Pictured here are some of the individuals featured in "I Am Today's Filipino," a photograph and video exhibit that lends a glimpse into the individual experiences that reflect the collective story of the Filipino community. The exhibit encourages a greater awareness of the many contributions that Filipinos in the United States have made and continue to make. It was created by Celina Taganas-Duffy and Ray Carbullido. (Photograph by and courtesy of Karlo David.)

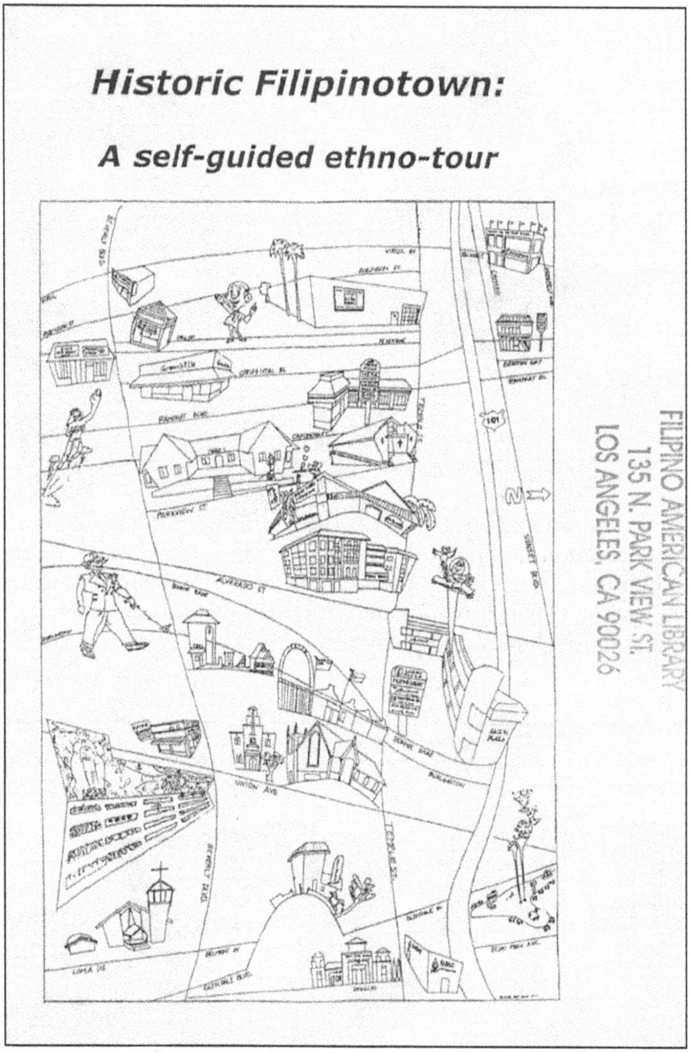

Historic Filipinotown:

A self-guided ethno-tour

During August 2006, in response to a high demand by the community to learn more about the history of Filipino Americans in Los Angeles, the Filipino American Library reestablished regular bus tours of the 2.1-square-mile area of Historic Filipinotown, where there are more than 25 Filipino American businesses, organizations, and landmarks. Pictured below is one of the original tours in the 1980s, led by community activist and former UCLA professor "Uncle Roy" Morales. (Courtesy of the Filipino American Library.)

SUBSTITUTE Item 73

MOTION

The City of Los Angeles comprises a variety of communities that make up our rich existence as a multi-cultural metropolis. The City has recognized this for many years and has periodically designated certain geographic areas with names based upon historical significance, current cultural attributes, location and other unique characteristics.

Within Council District 13 there is a significant population of persons of Filipino ancestry and Filipino-Americans who call the district home. In particular, there is a high concentration of persons of Filipino ancestry in the area commonly referred to as the Temple-Beverly corridor. Today, persons of Filipino background comprise the second largest group of Asian origin people in Los Angeles County with 261,794 residing in the county.

Within this corridor and its proximity, there are several Filipino businesses, restaurants, churches, community organizations, social services, and health clinics. It is a community of Filipino homeowners and renters as well.

Several residents, community members, and community organizations have requested the City to officially designate a specific area as "Historic Filipinotown". Council District 13 has worked with key residents, community members, and organizations to form an "Historic Filipinotown" Committee to look at the official designation of an "Historic Filipinotown." This effort has included reaching out to the community through community consultative groups to receive their reaction and vision of an "Historic Filipinotown." There has been overwhelming support by the community and a commitment to work towards the positive development of the area, once designated as "Historic Filipinotown."

In order to proceed with this designation, action is needed to approve it and to direct the Department of Public Works (Bureau of Engineering) and Department of Transportation to provide the necessary resources to implement the designation of "Historic Filipinotown."

I THEREFORE MOVE that the area bounded on the east by Glendale Boulevard, on the north by the 101 Freeway, on the west by Hoover Street, and the south by Beverly Boulevard be designated as "Historic Filipinotown."

I FURTHER MOVE that the Department of Public Works be directed to implement the designation of "Historic Filipinotown."

I FURTHER MOVE that the Department of Transportation be instructed to design and install signs at appropriate locations in order to identify "Historic Filipinotown."

PRESENTED BY: *E. G.H.*
ERIC GARCETTI
Councilmember, 13th District

SECONDED BY: *(signature)*

On August 2, 2002, the City of Los Angeles formally recognized the historical and cultural contributions of Filipino Angelenos by designating the Temple-Beverly corridor, just west of downtown, as Historic Filipinotown. Over 100 community leaders, Filipino veterans, students, city workers, and Los Angeles residents gathered at city hall to witness the dedication. (Courtesy of Chito Tenza.)

Here is the City of Angels in 2006, as seen through the lens of Karlo David, a professional Filipino photographer who often shoots community events. Today Los Angeles is the most populous city in the state of California, and 260,158 of its residents are of Filipino ancestry (according to the 2000 Census). An estimated 6,900 of those people live in the recently designated area of Historic Filipinotown.

This photograph is provided by Filipino American businessman Chito Tenza, a former staff member in councilmember Eric Garcetti's office and former president of the Historic Filipinotown Chamber of Commerce. City and community leaders hold the eight-foot-long, blue Historic Filipinotown sign—the longest sign in the history of the city of Los Angeles, which was installed at Temple Street and Union Avenue. Another sign off Highway 101 directs motorists to the designated Filipino community, which is bordered by Hoover Street on the west, Glendale Boulevard to the east, Highway 101 to the north, and Beverly Boulevard on the south. "Filipinos are one of the strongest ethnic communities in Southern California," said former Los Angeles mayor James Hahn, who attended the August 2002 dedication wearing a white *barong Tagalog*, the national dress of the Philippines. "This is long overdue."

BIBLIOGRAPHY

Bulosan, Carlos. *America is in the Heart.* Harcourt, Brace, and Company, 1943.

Corpus, Severino F. *An Analysis of the Racial Adjustment Activities and Problems of the Filipino-American Christian Fellowship in Los Angeles.* 1938 thesis at the University of Southern California. Reprinted in 1975 by Rand E. Research Associates.

Crouchett, Lorraine Jacobs. *Filipinos in California from the Days of the Galleons to the Present.* Downey Place Publishing House, 1982.

Dia, Paul. *Conflict & Controversy in Urban Development, The Filipino Community in the Greater Los Angeles Area.* 2003. http://www.lmu.edu/csla/community/students_projects/philipino/

España-Maram, Linda. *Creating Masculinity in Los Angeles's Little Manila.* Columbia University Press, 2006.

http://personal.anderson.ucla.edu/eloisa.borah/filfaqs.htm

http://www.apa.si.edu/filamcentennial/timeline.html

http://www.fasgi.org/news

http://www.filipinoamericanlibrary.org/

http://www.yo-yo.com

Historic Filipinotown "ethno-tour" document, Filipino American Library

Magalong, Michelle deGuzman. *The Search for "P-town": Filipino American Place(s) in Los Angeles.* Critical Planning, Summer 2003.

Mayberry, Jodine. *Filipinos.* Visual Education Corporation, 1990.

Motoyoshi, Michelle. *Filipinos in California.* Toucan Valley Publications, Inc., 1999.

Noriega, Violeta A. *Pilipino Proverbs.* Philippine Cultural and Educational Services, 1998.

The Philippine Progress Weekly Magazine. December 15, 1927.

Visit us at
arcadiapublishing.com

www.ingramcontent.com/pod-product-compliance
Lightning Source LLC
Chambersburg PA
CBHW080630110426
42813CB00006B/1650